CHARITIES ACT 2006 (UK)

Updated as of March 26, 2018

THE LAW LIBRARY

TABLE OF CONTENTS

Introductory Text	4
Part 1. Meaning of "charity" and "charitable purpose"	4
Part 2. Regulation of charities	5
Part 3. Funding for charitable, benevolent or philanthropic institutions	11
Part 4. Miscellaneous and general	30
Schedules	37
Schedule 1. The Charity Commission	37
Schedule 2. Establishment of the Charity Commission: supplementary	37
Schedule 3. The Charity Tribunal	37
Schedule 4. Appeals and applications to Charity Tribunal	37
Schedule 5. Exempt charities: increased regulation under 1993 Act	38
Schedule 6. Group accounts	38
Schedule 7. Charitable incorporated organisations	38
Schedule 8. Minor and consequential amendments	38
Schedule 9. Repeals and revocations	62
Schedule 10. Transitional provisions and savings	64
Open Government Licence v3.0	68

Introductory Text

Charities Act 2006

2006 CHAPTER 50

An Act to provide for the establishment and functions of the Charity Commission for England and Wales and the Charity Tribunal; to make other amendments of the law about charities, including provision about charitable incorporated organisations; to make further provision about public charitable collections and other fund-raising carried on in connection with charities and other institutions; to make other provision about the funding of such institutions; and for connected purposes.
[8th November 2006]
Be it enacted by the Queen's most Excellent Majesty, by and with the advice and consent of the Lords Spiritual and Temporal, and Commons, in this present Parliament assembled, and by the authority of the same, as follows:—

Part 1. Meaning of "charity" and "charitable purpose"

Part 1. Meaning of "charity" and "charitable purpose"

F11. Meaning of "charity"

. . . .
Amendments (Textual)
F1. Ss. 1-9 repealed (14.3.2012) by Charities Act 2011 (c. 25), s. 355, Sch. 10 (with s. 20. (2), Sch. 8)

F12. Meaning of "charitable purpose"

. . . .
Amendments (Textual)
F1. Ss. 1-9 repealed (14.3.2012) by Charities Act 2011 (c. 25), s. 355, Sch. 10 (with s. 20. (2), Sch. 8)

F13. The "public benefit" test

. . . .
Amendments (Textual)

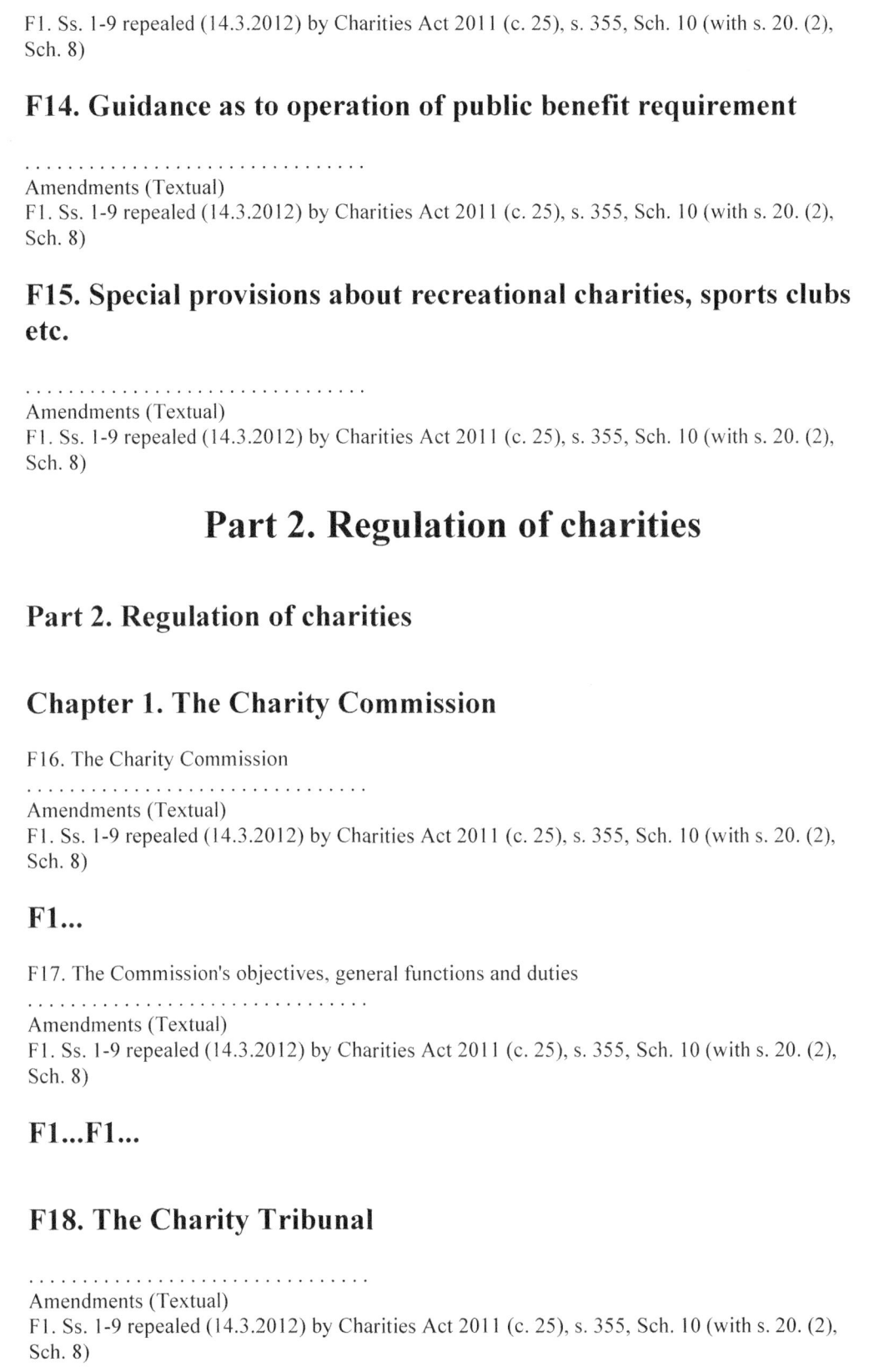

F1. Ss. 1-9 repealed (14.3.2012) by Charities Act 2011 (c. 25), s. 355, Sch. 10 (with s. 20. (2), Sch. 8)

F14. Guidance as to operation of public benefit requirement

....
Amendments (Textual)
F1. Ss. 1-9 repealed (14.3.2012) by Charities Act 2011 (c. 25), s. 355, Sch. 10 (with s. 20. (2), Sch. 8)

F15. Special provisions about recreational charities, sports clubs etc.

....
Amendments (Textual)
F1. Ss. 1-9 repealed (14.3.2012) by Charities Act 2011 (c. 25), s. 355, Sch. 10 (with s. 20. (2), Sch. 8)

Part 2. Regulation of charities

Part 2. Regulation of charities

Chapter 1. The Charity Commission

F16. The Charity Commission
....
Amendments (Textual)
F1. Ss. 1-9 repealed (14.3.2012) by Charities Act 2011 (c. 25), s. 355, Sch. 10 (with s. 20. (2), Sch. 8)

F1...

F17. The Commission's objectives, general functions and duties
....
Amendments (Textual)
F1. Ss. 1-9 repealed (14.3.2012) by Charities Act 2011 (c. 25), s. 355, Sch. 10 (with s. 20. (2), Sch. 8)

F1...F1...

F18. The Charity Tribunal

....
Amendments (Textual)
F1. Ss. 1-9 repealed (14.3.2012) by Charities Act 2011 (c. 25), s. 355, Sch. 10 (with s. 20. (2), Sch. 8)

Chapter 3. Registration of charities

F19. Registration of charities
. . . .
Amendments (Textual)
F1. Ss. 1-9 repealed (14.3.2012) by Charities Act 2011 (c. 25), s. 355, Sch. 10 (with s. 20. (2), Sch. 8)
10. Interim changes in threshold for registration of small charities
(1) At any time before the appointed day, the Minister may by order amend section 3 of the 1993 Act (the register of charities) so as to—
    (a) replace section 3. (5)(c) (threshold for registration of small charities) with a provision referring to a charity whose gross income does not exceed such sum as is prescribed in the order, and
    (b) define "gross income" for the purposes of that provision.
(2) Subsection (1) does not affect the existing power under section 3. (12) of that Act to increase the financial limit specified in section 3. (5)(c).
(3) This section ceases to have effect on the appointed day.
(4) In this section "the appointed day" means the day on which section 3. A(1) to (5) of the 1993 Act (as substituted by section 9 of this Act) come into force by virtue of an order under section 79 of this Act.
Commencement Information
I1. S. 10 in force at 27.2.2007 by S.I. 2007/309, art. 2, Sch.

Exempt charities: registration and regulation

F211. Changes in exempt charities
. . . .
Amendments (Textual)
F2. Ss. 11-44 repealed (14.3.2012) by Charities Act 2011 (c. 25), s. 355, Sch. 10 (with s. 20. (2), Sch. 8)
F212. Increased regulation of exempt charities under 1993 Act
. . . .
Amendments (Textual)
F2. Ss. 11-44 repealed (14.3.2012) by Charities Act 2011 (c. 25), s. 355, Sch. 10 (with s. 20. (2), Sch. 8)
F213. General duty of principal regulator in relation to exempt charity
. . . .
Amendments (Textual)
F2. Ss. 11-44 repealed (14.3.2012) by Charities Act 2011 (c. 25), s. 355, Sch. 10 (with s. 20. (2), Sch. 8)
F214. Commission to consult principal regulator before exercising powers in relation to exempt charity
. . . .
Amendments (Textual)
F2. Ss. 11-44 repealed (14.3.2012) by Charities Act 2011 (c. 25), s. 355, Sch. 10 (with s. 20. (2), Sch. 8)

Chapter 4. Application of property cy-près

15. F2...

....
Amendments (Textual)
F2. Ss. 11-44 repealed (14.3.2012) by Charities Act 2011 (c. 25), s. 355, Sch. 10 (with s. 20. (2), Sch. 8)

16. F2...
....
Amendments (Textual)
F2. Ss. 11-44 repealed (14.3.2012) by Charities Act 2011 (c. 25), s. 355, Sch. 10 (with s. 20. (2), Sch. 8)

17. F2...
....
Amendments (Textual)
F2. Ss. 11-44 repealed (14.3.2012) by Charities Act 2011 (c. 25), s. 355, Sch. 10 (with s. 20. (2), Sch. 8)

Schemes

18. F2...
....
Amendments (Textual)
F2. Ss. 11-44 repealed (14.3.2012) by Charities Act 2011 (c. 25), s. 355, Sch. 10 (with s. 20. (2), Sch. 8)

Chapter 5. +N.I.Assistance and supervision of charities by court and Commission

19. F2...
....
Amendments (Textual)
F2. Ss. 11-44 repealed (14.3.2012) by Charities Act 2011 (c. 25), s. 355, Sch. 10 (with s. 20. (2), Sch. 8)

Directions by Commission

20. F2...
....
Amendments (Textual)
F2. Ss. 11-44 repealed (14.3.2012) by Charities Act 2011 (c. 25), s. 355, Sch. 10 (with s. 20. (2), Sch. 8)

21. F2...
....
Amendments (Textual)
F2. Ss. 11-44 repealed (14.3.2012) by Charities Act 2011 (c. 25), s. 355, Sch. 10 (with s. 20. (2), Sch. 8)

Publicity relating to schemes

22. F2...
....
Amendments (Textual)
F2. Ss. 11-44 repealed (14.3.2012) by Charities Act 2011 (c. 25), s. 355, Sch. 10 (with s. 20. (2),

Sch. 8)

Common investment schemes+N.I.

23. F2...+N.I.
....
Amendments (Textual)
F2. Ss. 11-44 repealed (14.3.2012) by Charities Act 2011 (c. 25), s. 355, Sch. 10 (with s. 20. (2), Sch. 8)

Advice or other assistance

24. F2...
....
Amendments (Textual)
F2. Ss. 11-44 repealed (14.3.2012) by Charities Act 2011 (c. 25), s. 355, Sch. 10 (with s. 20. (2), Sch. 8)
25. F2...
....
Amendments (Textual)
F2. Ss. 11-44 repealed (14.3.2012) by Charities Act 2011 (c. 25), s. 355, Sch. 10 (with s. 20. (2), Sch. 8)

Powers of entry etc.

26. F2...
....
Amendments (Textual)
F2. Ss. 11-44 repealed (14.3.2012) by Charities Act 2011 (c. 25), s. 355, Sch. 10 (with s. 20. (2), Sch. 8)

Mortgages of charity land

27. F2...
....
Amendments (Textual)
F2. Ss. 11-44 repealed (14.3.2012) by Charities Act 2011 (c. 25), s. 355, Sch. 10 (with s. 20. (2), Sch. 8)

Chapter 6. Audit or examination of accounts where charity is not a company

28. F2...

....
Amendments (Textual)
F2. Ss. 11-44 repealed (14.3.2012) by Charities Act 2011 (c. 25), s. 355, Sch. 10 (with s. 20. (2), Sch. 8)

29. F2...

....
Amendments (Textual)
F2. Ss. 11-44 repealed (14.3.2012) by Charities Act 2011 (c. 25), s. 355, Sch. 10 (with s. 20. (2), Sch. 8)

30. F2...

....
Amendments (Textual)
F2. Ss. 11-44 repealed (14.3.2012) by Charities Act 2011 (c. 25), s. 355, Sch. 10 (with s. 20. (2), Sch. 8)

Chapter 7. Charitable companies

31. F2...

....
Amendments (Textual)
F2. Ss. 11-44 repealed (14.3.2012) by Charities Act 2011 (c. 25), s. 355, Sch. 10 (with s. 20. (2), Sch. 8)

32. F2...

....
Amendments (Textual)
F2. Ss. 11-44 repealed (14.3.2012) by Charities Act 2011 (c. 25), s. 355, Sch. 10 (with s. 20. (2), Sch. 8)

33. F2...

....
Amendments (Textual)
F2. Ss. 11-44 repealed (14.3.2012) by Charities Act 2011 (c. 25), s. 355, Sch. 10 (with s. 20. (2), Sch. 8)

Chapter 8. Charitable incorporated organisations

34. F2...

....
Amendments (Textual)
F2. Ss. 11-44 repealed (14.3.2012) by Charities Act 2011 (c. 25), s. 355, Sch. 10 (with s. 20. (2), Sch. 8)

Chapter 9. Charity trustees etc.

35. F2...
. . . .
Amendments (Textual)
F2. Ss. 11-44 repealed (14.3.2012) by Charities Act 2011 (c. 25), s. 355, Sch. 10 (with s. 20. (2), Sch. 8)

Remuneration of trustees etc.

36. F2...
. . . .
Amendments (Textual)
F2. Ss. 11-44 repealed (14.3.2012) by Charities Act 2011 (c. 25), s. 355, Sch. 10 (with s. 20. (2), Sch. 8)
37. F2...
. . . .
Amendments (Textual)
F2. Ss. 11-44 repealed (14.3.2012) by Charities Act 2011 (c. 25), s. 355, Sch. 10 (with s. 20. (2), Sch. 8)

Liability of trustees etc.

38. F2...
. . . .
Amendments (Textual)
F2. Ss. 11-44 repealed (14.3.2012) by Charities Act 2011 (c. 25), s. 355, Sch. 10 (with s. 20. (2), Sch. 8)
39. F2...
. . . .
Amendments (Textual)
F2. Ss. 11-44 repealed (14.3.2012) by Charities Act 2011 (c. 25), s. 355, Sch. 10 (with s. 20. (2), Sch. 8)

Chapter 10. Powers of unincorporated charities

40. F2...

. . . .
Amendments (Textual)
F2. Ss. 11-44 repealed (14.3.2012) by Charities Act 2011 (c. 25), s. 355, Sch. 10 (with s. 20. (2), Sch. 8)

41. F2...

. . . .
Amendments (Textual)
F2. Ss. 11-44 repealed (14.3.2012) by Charities Act 2011 (c. 25), s. 355, Sch. 10 (with s. 20. (2), Sch. 8)

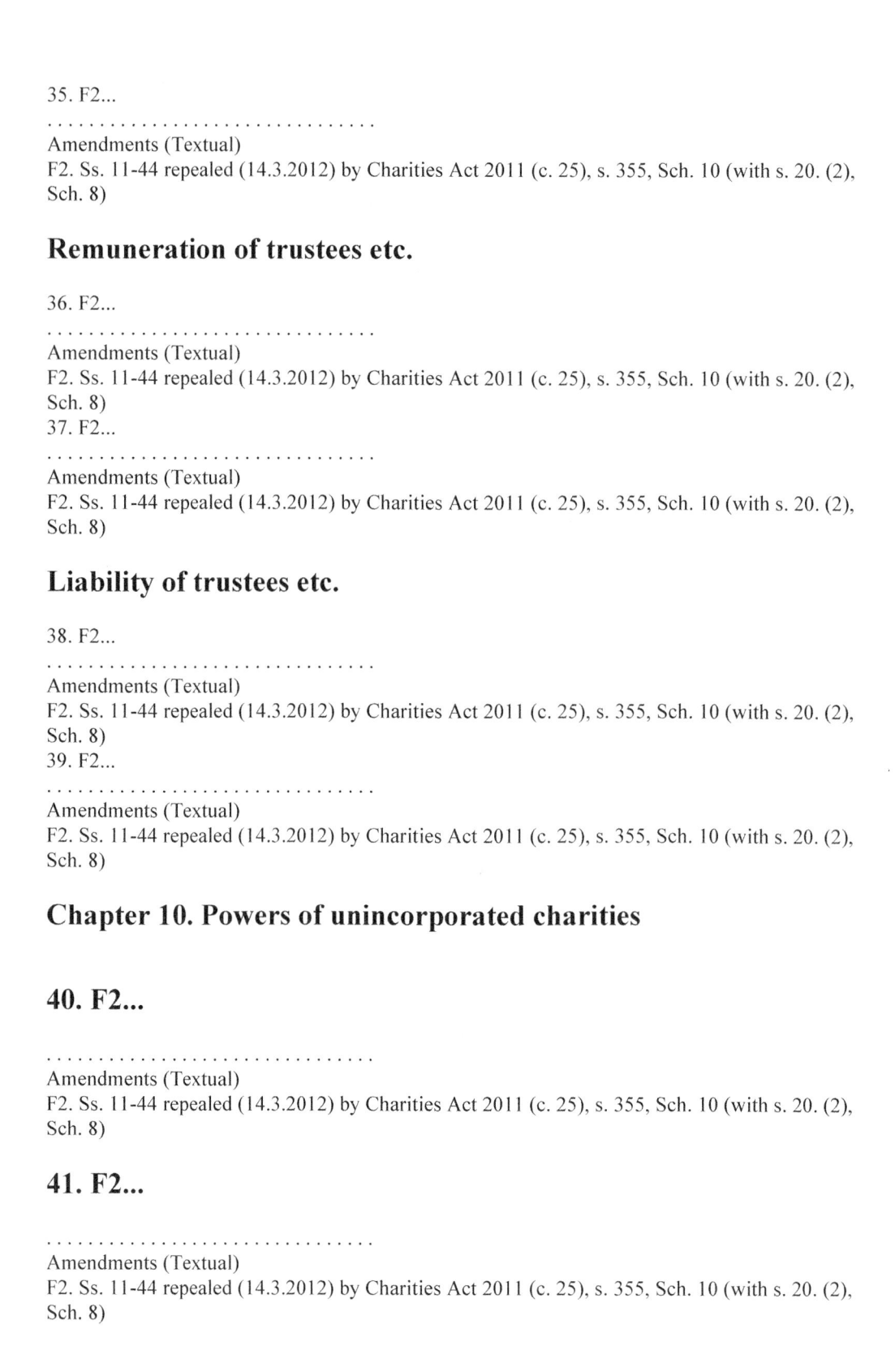

42. F2...

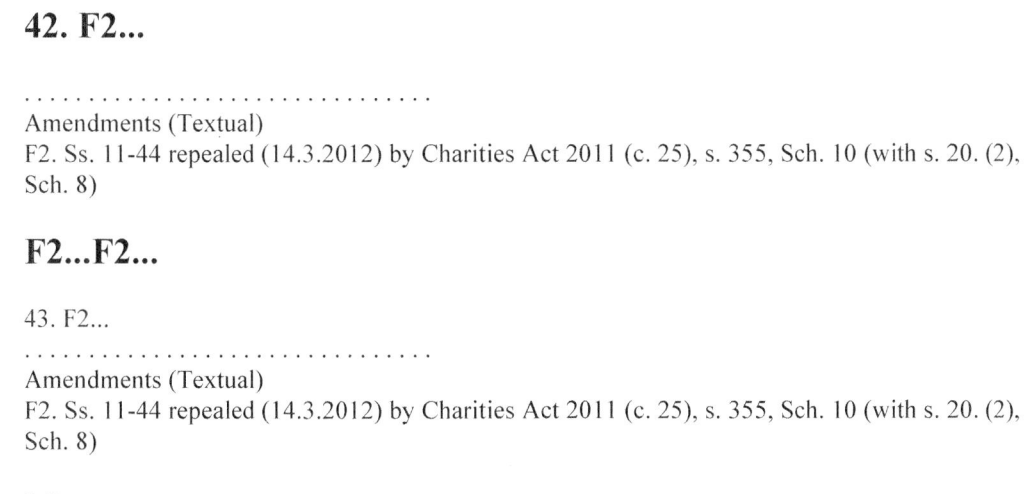

....
Amendments (Textual)
F2. Ss. 11-44 repealed (14.3.2012) by Charities Act 2011 (c. 25), s. 355, Sch. 10 (with s. 20. (2), Sch. 8)

F2...F2...

43. F2...
....
Amendments (Textual)
F2. Ss. 11-44 repealed (14.3.2012) by Charities Act 2011 (c. 25), s. 355, Sch. 10 (with s. 20. (2), Sch. 8)

Mergers

F244. Merger of charities
....
Amendments (Textual)
F2. Ss. 11-44 repealed (14.3.2012) by Charities Act 2011 (c. 25), s. 355, Sch. 10 (with s. 20. (2), Sch. 8)

Part 3. Funding for charitable, benevolent or philanthropic institutions

Part 3 Funding for charitable, benevolent or philanthropic institutions

Chapter 1. Public charitable collections

Modifications etc. (not altering text)
C1. Pt. 3 Ch. 1 power to amend or modify conferred by 1993 c. 10, Sch. 1. C, paras. 6, 7 (as inserted (27.2.2007) by Charities Act 2006 (c. 50), s. 79. (2), Sch. 4; S.I. 2007/309, art. 2, Sch.)
45. Regulation of public charitable collections
(1) This Chapter regulates public charitable collections, which are of the following two types—
   (a) collections in a public place; and
   (b) door to door collections.
(2) For the purposes of this Chapter—
   (a) "public charitable collection" means (subject to section 46) a charitable appeal which is made—
(i) in any public place, or
(ii) by means of visits to houses or business premises (or both);
   (b) "charitable appeal" means an appeal to members of the public which is—
(i) an appeal to them to give money or other property, or
(ii) an appeal falling within subsection (4),
(or both) and which is made in association with a representation that the whole or any part of its

proceeds is to be applied for charitable, benevolent or philanthropic purposes;

(c) a "collection in a public place" is a public charitable collection that is made in a public place, as mentioned in paragraph (a)(i);

(d) a "door to door collection" is a public charitable collection that is made by means of visits to houses or business premises (or both), as mentioned in paragraph (a)(ii).

(3) For the purposes of subsection (2)(b)—

(a) the reference to the giving of money is to doing so by whatever means; and

(b) it does not matter whether the giving of money or other property is for consideration or otherwise.

(4) An appeal falls within this subsection if it consists in or includes—

(a) the making of an offer to sell goods or to supply services, or

(b) the exposing of goods for sale,

to members of the public.

(5) In this section—

"business premises" means any premises used for business or other commercial purposes;

"house" includes any part of a building constituting a separate dwelling;

"public place" means—

- any highway, and

- (subject to subsection (6)) any other place to which, at any time when the appeal is made, members of the public have or are permitted to have access and which either—

is not within a building, or

if within a building, is a public area within any station, airport or shopping precinct or any other similar public area.

(6) In subsection (5), paragraph (b) of the definition of "public place" does not include—

(a) any place to which members of the public are permitted to have access only if any payment or ticket required as a condition of access has been made or purchased; or

(b) any place to which members of the public are permitted to have access only by virtue of permission given for the purposes of the appeal in question.

Commencement Information

I1. S. 45. (2)-(6) in force at 1.4.2008 for specified purposes by S.I. 2007/3286, art. 3, Sch. 2 (with art. 4)

46. Charitable appeals that are not public charitable collections

(1) A charitable appeal is not a public charitable collection if the appeal—

(a) is made in the course of a public meeting; or

(b) is made—

(i) on land within a churchyard or burial ground contiguous or adjacent to a place of public worship, or

(ii) on other land occupied for the purposes of a place of public worship and contiguous or adjacent to it,

where the land is enclosed or substantially enclosed (whether by any wall or building or otherwise); or

(c) is made on land to which members of the public have access only—

(i) by virtue of the express or implied permission of the occupier of the land, or

(ii) by virtue of any enactment,

and the occupier is the promoter of the collection; or

(d) is an appeal to members of the public to give money or other property by placing it in an unattended receptacle.

(2) For the purposes of subsection (1)(c) "the occupier", in relation to unoccupied land, means the person entitled to occupy it.

(3) For the purposes of subsection (1)(d) a receptacle is unattended if it is not in the possession or custody of a person acting as a collector.

Commencement Information

I2. S. 46 in force at 1.4.2008 for specified purposes by S.I. 2007/3286, art. 3, Sch. 2 (with art. 4)

47. Other definitions for purposes of this Chapter
(1) In this Chapter—
"charitable, benevolent or philanthropic institution" means—
- a charity, or
- an institution (other than a charity) which is established for charitable, benevolent, or philanthropic purposes;
"collector", in relation to a public charitable collection, means any person by whom the appeal in question is made (whether made by him alone or with others and whether made by him for remuneration or otherwise);
"local authority" means a unitary authority, the council of a district so far as it is not a unitary authority, the council of a London borough or of a Welsh county or county borough, the Common Council of the City of London or the Council of the Isles of Scilly;
"prescribed" means prescribed by regulations under section 63;
"proceeds", in relation to a public charitable collection, means all money or other property given (whether for consideration or otherwise) in response to the charitable appeal in question;
"promoter", in relation to a public charitable collection, means—
- a person who (whether alone or with others and whether for remuneration or otherwise) organises or controls the conduct of the charitable appeal in question, or
- where there is no person acting as mentioned in paragraph (a), any person who acts as a collector in respect of the collection,
and associated expressions are to be construed accordingly;
"public collections certificate" means a certificate issued by the Commission under section 52.
(2) In subsection (1) "unitary authority" means—
　(a) the council of a county so far as it is the council for an area for which there are no district councils;
　(b) the council of any district comprised in an area for which there is no county council.
(3) The functions exercisable under this Chapter by a local authority are to be exercisable—
　(a) as respects the Inner Temple, by its Sub-Treasurer, and
　(b) as respects the Middle Temple, by its Under Treasurer;
and references in this Chapter to a local authority or to the area of a local authority are to be construed accordingly.
Commencement Information
I3. S. 47. (1) in force at 1.4.2008 for specified purposes by S.I. 2007/3286, art. 3, Sch. 2 (with art. 4)
Prospective

Restrictions on conducting collections

48. Restrictions on conducting collections in a public place
(1) A collection in a public place must not be conducted unless—
　(a) the promoters of the collection hold a public collections certificate in force under section 52 in respect of the collection, and
　(b) the collection is conducted in accordance with a permit issued under section 59 by the local authority in whose area it is conducted.
(2) Subsection (1) does not apply to a public charitable collection which is an exempt collection by virtue of section 50 (local, short-term collections).
(3) Where—
　(a) a collection in a public place is conducted in contravention of subsection (1), and
　(b) the circumstances of the case do not fall within section 50. (6),
every promoter of the collection is guilty of an offence and liable on summary conviction to a fine not exceeding level 5 on the standard scale.
49. Restrictions on conducting door to door collections

(1) A door to door collection must not be conducted unless the promoters of the collection—
    (a) hold a public collections certificate in force under section 52 in respect of the collection, and
    (b) have within the prescribed period falling before the day (or the first of the days) on which the collection takes place—
(i) notified the local authority in whose area the collection is to be conducted of the matters mentioned in subsection (3), and
(ii) provided that authority with a copy of the certificate mentioned in paragraph (a).
(2) Subsection (1) does not apply to a door to door collection which is an exempt collection by virtue of section 50 (local, short-term collections).
(3) The matters referred to in subsection (1)(b)(i) are—
    (a) the purpose for which the proceeds of the appeal are to be applied;
    (b) the prescribed particulars of when the collection is to be conducted;
    (c) the locality within which the collection is to be conducted; and
    (d) such other matters as may be prescribed.
(4) Where—
    (a) a door to door collection is conducted in contravention of subsection (1), and
    (b) the circumstances of the case do not fall within section 50. (6),
every promoter of the collection is guilty of an offence and liable on summary conviction to a fine not exceeding level 5 on the standard scale.
This is subject to subsection (5).
(5) Where—
    (a) a door to door collection is conducted in contravention of subsection (1),
    (b) the appeal is for goods only, and
    (c) the circumstances of the case do not fall within section 50. (6),
every promoter of the collection is guilty of an offence and liable on summary conviction to a fine not exceeding level 3 on the standard scale.
(6) In subsection (5) "goods" includes all personal chattels other than things in action and money.
50. Exemption for local, short-term collections
(1) A public charitable collection is an exempt collection if—
    (a) it is a local, short-term collection (see subsection (2)), and
    (b) the promoters notify the local authority in whose area it is to be conducted of the matters mentioned in subsection (3) within the prescribed period falling before the day (or the first of the days) on which the collection takes place,
unless, within the prescribed period beginning with the date when they are so notified, the local authority serve a notice under subsection (4) on the promoters.
(2) A public charitable collection is a local, short term collection if—
    (a) the appeal is local in character; and
    (b) the duration of the appeal does not exceed the prescribed period of time.
(3) The matters referred to in subsection (1)(b) are—
    (a) the purpose for which the proceeds of the appeal are to be applied;
    (b) the date or dates on which the collection is to be conducted;
    (c) the place at which, or the locality within which, the collection is to be conducted; and
    (d) such other matters as may be prescribed.
(4) Where it appears to the local authority—
    (a) that the collection is not a local, short-term collection, or
    (b) that the promoters or any of them have or has on any occasion—
(i) breached any provision of regulations made under section 63, or
(ii) been convicted of an offence within section 53. (2)(a)(i) to (v),
they must serve on the promoters written notice of their decision to that effect and the reasons for their decision.
(5) That notice must also state the right of appeal conferred by section 62. (1) and the time within which such an appeal must be brought.
(6) Where—

(a) a collection in a public place is conducted otherwise than in accordance with section 48. (1) or a door to door collection is conducted otherwise than in accordance with section 49. (1), and
(b) the collection is a local, short term collection but the promoters do not notify the local authority as mentioned in subsection (1)(b),
every promoter of the collection is guilty of an offence and liable on summary conviction to a fine not exceeding level 3 on the standard scale.
Prospective

Public collections certificates

51. Applications for certificates
(1) A person or persons proposing to promote public charitable collections (other than exempt collections) may apply to the Charity Commission for a public collections certificate in respect of those collections.
(2) The application must be made—
    (a) within the specified period falling before the first of the collections is to commence, or
    (b) before such later date as the Commission may allow in the case of that application.
(3) The application must—
    (a) be made in such form as may be specified,
    (b) specify the period for which the certificate is sought (which must be no more than 5 years), and
    (c) contain such other information as may be specified.
(4) An application under this section may be made for a public collections certificate in respect of a single collection; and the references in this Chapter, in the context of such certificates, to public charitable collections are to be read accordingly.
(5) In subsections (2) and (3) "specified" means specified in regulations made by the Commission after consulting such persons or bodies of persons as it considers appropriate.
(6) Regulations under subsection (5)—
    (a) must be published in such manner as the Commission considers appropriate,
    (b) may make different provision for different cases or descriptions of case, and
    (c) may make such incidental, supplementary, consequential or transitional provision as the Commission considers appropriate.
(7) In this section "exempt collection" means a public charitable collection which is an exempt collection by virtue of section 50.
52. Determination of applications and issue of certificates
(1) On receiving an application for a public collections certificate made in accordance with section 51, the Commission may make such inquiries (whether under section 54 or otherwise) as it thinks fit.
(2) The Commission must, after making any such inquiries, determine the application by either—
    (a) issuing a public collections certificate in respect of the collections, or
    (b) refusing the application on one or more of the grounds specified in section 53. (1).
(3) A public collections certificate—
    (a) must specify such matters as may be prescribed, and
    (b) shall (subject to section 56) be in force for—
(i) the period specified in the application in accordance with section 51. (3)(b), or
(ii) such shorter period as the Commission thinks fit.
(4) The Commission may, at the time of issuing a public collections certificate, attach to it such conditions as it thinks fit.
(5) Conditions attached under subsection (4) may include conditions prescribed for the purposes of that subsection.
(6) The Commission must secure that the terms of any conditions attached under subsection (4) are consistent with the provisions of any regulations under section 63 (whether or not prescribing

conditions for the purposes of that subsection).

(7) Where the Commission—

(a) refuses to issue a certificate, or

(b) attaches any condition to it,

it must serve on the applicant written notice of its decision and the reasons for its decision.

(8) That notice must also state the right of appeal conferred by section 57. (1) and the time within which such an appeal must be brought.

53. Grounds for refusing to issue a certificate

(1) The grounds on which the Commission may refuse an application for a public collections certificate are—

(a) that the applicant has been convicted of a relevant offence;

(b) where the applicant is a person other than a charitable, benevolent or philanthropic institution for whose benefit the collections are proposed to be conducted, that the Commission is not satisfied that the applicant is authorised (whether by any such institution or by any person acting on behalf of any such institution) to promote the collections;

(c) that it appears to the Commission that the applicant, in promoting any other collection authorised under this Chapter or under section 119 of the 1982 Act, failed to exercise the required due diligence;

(d) that the Commission is not satisfied that the applicant will exercise the required due diligence in promoting the proposed collections;

(e) that it appears to the Commission that the amount likely to be applied for charitable, benevolent or philanthropic purposes in consequence of the proposed collections would be inadequate, having regard to the likely amount of the proceeds of the collections;

(f) that it appears to the Commission that the applicant or any other person would be likely to receive an amount by way of remuneration in connection with the collections that would be excessive, having regard to all the circumstances;

(g) that the applicant has failed to provide information—

(i) required for the purposes of the application for the certificate or a previous application, or

(ii) in response to a request under section 54. (1);

(h) that it appears to the Commission that information so provided to it by the applicant is false or misleading in a material particular;

(i) that it appears to the Commission that the applicant or any person authorised by him—

(i) has breached any conditions attached to a previous public collections certificate, or

(ii) has persistently breached any conditions attached to a permit issued under section 59;

(j) that it appears to the Commission that the applicant or any person authorised by him has on any occasion breached any provision of regulations made under section 63. (1)(b).

(2) For the purposes of subsection (1)—

(a) a "relevant offence" is—

(i) an offence under section 5 of the 1916 Act;

(ii) an offence under the 1939 Act;

(iii) an offence under section 119 of the 1982 Act or regulations made under it;

(iv) an offence under this Chapter;

(v) an offence involving dishonesty; or

(vi) an offence of a kind the commission of which would, in the opinion of the Commission, be likely to be facilitated by the issuing to the applicant of a public collections certificate; and

(b) the "required due diligence" is due diligence—

(i) to secure that persons authorised by the applicant to act as collectors for the purposes of the collection were (or will be) fit and proper persons;

(ii) to secure that such persons complied (or will comply) with the provisions of regulations under section 63. (1)(b) of this Act or (as the case may be) section 119 of the 1982 Act; or

(iii) to prevent badges or certificates of authority being obtained by persons other than those the applicant had so authorised.

(3) Where an application for a certificate is made by more than one person, any reference to the

applicant in subsection (1) or (2) is to be construed as a reference to any of the applicants.

(4) Subject to subsections (5) and (6), the reference in subsection (2)(b)(iii) to badges or certificates of authority is a reference to badges or certificates of authority in a form prescribed by regulations under section 63. (1)(b) of this Act or (as the case may be) under section 119 of the 1982 Act.

(5) Subsection (2)(b) applies to the conduct of the applicant (or any of the applicants) in relation to any public charitable collection authorised—

    (a) under regulations made under section 5 of the 1916 Act (collection of money or sale of articles in a street or other public place), or

    (b) under the 1939 Act (collection of money or other property by means of visits from house to house),

as it applies to his conduct in relation to a collection authorised under this Chapter, but subject to the modifications set out in subsection (6).

(6) The modifications are—

    (a) in the case of a collection authorised under regulations made under the 1916 Act—

(i) the reference in subsection (2)(b)(ii) to regulations under section 63. (1)(b) of this Act is to be construed as a reference to the regulations under which the collection in question was authorised, and

(ii) the reference in subsection (2)(b)(iii) to badges or certificates of authority is to be construed as a reference to any written authority provided to a collector pursuant to those regulations; and

    (b) in the case of a collection authorised under the 1939 Act—

(i) the reference in subsection (2)(b)(ii) to regulations under section 63. (1)(b) of this Act is to be construed as a reference to regulations under section 4 of that Act, and

(ii) the reference in subsection (2)(b)(iii) to badges or certificates of authority is to be construed as a reference to badges or certificates of authority in a form prescribed by such regulations.

(7) In subsections (1)(c) and (5) a reference to a collection authorised under this Chapter is a reference to a public charitable collection that—

    (a) is conducted in accordance with section 48 or section 49 (as the case may be), or

    (b) is an exempt collection by virtue of section 50.

(8) In this section—

"the 1916 Act" means the Police, Factories, &c. (Miscellaneous Provisions) Act 1916 (c. 31);

"the 1939 Act" means the House to House Collections Act 1939 (c. 44); and

"the 1982 Act" means the Civic Government (Scotland) Act 1982 (c. 45).

54. Power to call for information and documents

(1) The Commission may request—

    (a) any applicant for a public collections certificate, or

    (b) any person to whom such a certificate has been issued,

to provide it with any information in his possession, or document in his custody or under this control, which is relevant to the exercise of any of its functions under this Chapter.

(2) Nothing in this section affects the power conferred on the Commission by [F1section 52 of the Charities Act 2011].

Amendments (Textual)

F1. Words in s. 54. (2) substituted (14.3.2012) by Charities Act 2011 (c. 25), s. 355, Sch. 7 para. 118 (with s. 20. (2), Sch. 8)

55. Transfer of certificate between trustees of unincorporated charity

(1) One or more individuals to whom a public collections certificate has been issued ("the holders") may apply to the Commission for a direction that the certificate be transferred to one or more other individuals ("the recipients").

(2) An application under subsection (1) must—

    (a) be in such form as may be specified, and

    (b) contain such information as may be specified.

(3) The Commission may direct that the certificate be transferred if it is satisfied that—

    (a) each of the holders is or was a trustee of a charity which is not a body corporate;

(b) each of the recipients is a trustee of that charity and consents to the transfer; and
(c) the charity trustees consent to the transfer.
(4) Where the Commission refuses to direct that a certificate be transferred, it must serve on the holders written notice of—
(a) its decision, and
(b) the reasons for its decision.
(5) That notice must also state the right of appeal conferred by section 57. (2) and the time within which such an appeal must be brought.
(6) Subsections (5) and (6) of section 51 apply for the purposes of subsection (2) of this section as they apply for the purposes of subsection (3) of that section.
(7) Except as provided by this section, a public collections certificate is not transferable.
56. Withdrawal or variation etc. of certificates
(1) Where subsection (2), (3) or (4) applies, the Commission may—
(a) withdraw a public collections certificate,
(b) suspend such a certificate,
(c) attach any condition (or further condition) to such a certificate, or
(d) vary any existing condition of such a certificate.
(2) This subsection applies where the Commission—
(a) has reason to believe there has been a change in the circumstances which prevailed at the time when it issued the certificate, and
(b) is of the opinion that, if the application for the certificate had been made in the new circumstances, it would not have issued the certificate or would have issued it subject to different or additional conditions.
(3) This subsection applies where—
(a) the holder of a certificate has unreasonably refused to provide any information or document in response to a request under section 54. (1), or
(b) the Commission has reason to believe that information provided to it by the holder of a certificate (or, where there is more than one holder, by any of them) for the purposes of the application for the certificate, or in response to such a request, was false or misleading in a material particular.
(4) This subsection applies where the Commission has reason to believe that there has been or is likely to be a breach of any condition of a certificate, or that a breach of such a condition is continuing.
(5) Any condition imposed at any time by the Commission under subsection (1) (whether by attaching a new condition to the certificate or by varying an existing condition) must be one that it would be appropriate for the Commission to attach to the certificate under section 52. (4) if the holder was applying for it in the circumstances prevailing at that time.
(6) The exercise by the Commission of the power conferred by paragraph (b), (c) or (d) of subsection (1) on one occasion does not prevent it from exercising any of the powers conferred by that subsection on a subsequent occasion; and on any subsequent occasion the reference in subsection (2)(a) to the time when the Commission issued the certificate is a reference to the time when it last exercised any of those powers.
(7) Where the Commission—
(a) withdraws or suspends a certificate,
(b) attaches a condition to a certificate, or
(c) varies an existing condition of a certificate,
it must serve on the holder written notice of its decision and the reasons for its decision.
(8) That notice must also state the right of appeal conferred by section 57. (3) and the time within which such an appeal must be brought.
(9) If the Commission—
(a) considers that the interests of the public require a decision by it under this section to have immediate effect, and
(b) includes a statement to that effect and the reasons for it in the notice served under subsection

(7),
the decision takes effect when that notice is served on the holder.
(10) In any other case the certificate shall continue to have effect as if it had not been withdrawn or suspended or (as the case may be) as if the condition had not been attached or varied—
   (a) until the time for bringing an appeal under section 57. (3) has expired, or
   (b) if such an appeal is duly brought, until the determination or abandonment of the appeal.
(11) A certificate suspended under this section shall (subject to any appeal and any withdrawal of the certificate) remain suspended until—
   (a) such time as the Commission may by notice direct that the certificate is again in force, or
   (b) the end of the period of six months beginning with the date on which the suspension takes effect,
whichever is the sooner.

57. Appeals against decisions of the Commission
(1) A person who has duly applied to the Commission for a public collections certificate may appeal to the [F2. Tribunal] against a decision of the Commission under section 52—
   (a) to refuse to issue the certificate, or
   (b) to attach any condition to it.
(2) A person to whom a public collections certificate has been issued may appeal to the Tribunal against a decision of the Commission not to direct that the certificate be transferred under section 55.
(3) A person to whom a public collections certificate has been issued may appeal to the Tribunal against a decision of the Commission under section 56—
   (a) to withdraw or suspend the certificate,
   (b) to attach a condition to the certificate, or
   (c) to vary an existing condition of the certificate.
(4) The Attorney General may appeal to the Tribunal against a decision of the Commission—
   (a) to issue, or to refuse to issue, a certificate,
   (b) to attach, or not to attach, any condition to a certificate (whether under section 52 or section 56),
   (c) to direct, or not to direct, that a certificate be transferred under section 55,
   (d) to withdraw or suspend, or not to withdraw or suspend, a certificate, or
   (e) to vary, or not to vary, an existing condition of a certificate.
(5) In determining an appeal under this section, the Tribunal—
   (a) must consider afresh the decision appealed against, and
   (b) may take into account evidence which was not available to the Commission.
(6) On an appeal under this section, the Tribunal may—
   (a) dismiss the appeal,
   (b) quash the decision, or
   (c) substitute for the decision another decision of a kind that the Commission could have made;
and in any case the Tribunal may give such directions as it thinks fit, having regard to the provisions of this Chapter and of regulations under section 63.
(7) If the Tribunal quashes the decision, it may remit the matter to the Commission (either generally or for determination in accordance with a finding made or direction given by the Tribunal).
[F3. (8)In this section "the Tribunal", in relation to any appeal under this section, means—
   (a) the Upper Tribunal, in any case where it is determined by or under Tribunal Procedure Rules that the Upper Tribunal is to hear the appeal; or
   (b) the First-tier Tribunal, in any other case;]

Amendments (Textual)
F2. Word in s. 57. (1) substituted (1.9.2009) by The Transfer of Functions of the Charity Tribunal Order 2009 (S.I. 2009/1834), art. 1, Sch. 1 para. 17. (a) (with Sch. 4)
F3. S. 57. (8) inserted (1.9.2009) by The Transfer of Functions of the Charity Tribunal Order 2009 (S.I. 2009/1834), art. 1, Sch. 1 para. 17. (b) (with Sch. 4)

Prospective

Permits

58. Applications for permits to conduct collections in public places

(1) A person or persons proposing to promote a collection in a public place (other than an exempt collection) in the area of a local authority may apply to the authority for a permit to conduct that collection.

(2) The application must be made within the prescribed period falling before the day (or the first of the days) on which the collection is to take place, except as provided in subsection (4).

(3) The application must—

(a) specify the date or dates in respect of which it is desired that the permit, if issued, should have effect (which, in the case of two or more dates, must not span a period of more than 12 months);

(b) be accompanied by a copy of the public collections certificate in force under section 52 in respect of the proposed collection; and

(c) contain such information as may be prescribed.

(4) Where an application ("the certificate application") has been made in accordance with section 51 for a public collections certificate in respect of the collection and either—

(a) the certificate application has not been determined by the end of the period mentioned in subsection (2) above, or

(b) the certificate application has been determined by the issue of such a certificate but at a time when there is insufficient time remaining for the application mentioned in subsection (2) ("the permit application") to be made by the end of that period,

the permit application must be made as early as practicable before the day (or the first of the days) on which the collection is to take place.

(5) In this section "exempt collection" means a collection in a public place which is an exempt collection by virtue of section 50.

59. Determination of applications and issue of permits

(1) On receiving an application made in accordance with section 58 for a permit in respect of a collection in a public place, a local authority must determine the application within the prescribed period by either—

(a) issuing a permit in respect of the collection, or

(b) refusing the application on the ground specified in section 60. (1).

(2) Where a local authority issue such a permit, it shall (subject to section 61) have effect in respect of the date or dates specified in the application in accordance with section 58. (3)(a).

(3) At the time of issuing a permit under this section, a local authority may attach to it such conditions within paragraphs (a) to (d) below as they think fit, having regard to the local circumstances of the collection—

(a) conditions specifying the day of the week, date, time or frequency of the collection;

(b) conditions specifying the locality or localities within their area in which the collection may be conducted;

(c) conditions regulating the manner in which the collection is to be conducted;

(d) such other conditions as may be prescribed for the purposes of this subsection.

(4) A local authority must secure that the terms of any conditions attached under subsection (3) are consistent with the provisions of any regulations under section 63 (whether or not prescribing conditions for the purposes of that subsection).

(5) Where a local authority—

(a) refuse to issue a permit, or

(b) attach any condition to it,

they must serve on the applicant written notice of their decision and the reasons for their decision.

(6) That notice must also state the right of appeal conferred by section 62. (2) and the time within

which such an appeal must be brought.

60. Refusal of permits

(1) The only ground on which a local authority may refuse an application for a permit to conduct a collection in a public place is that it appears to them that the collection would cause undue inconvenience to members of the public by reason of—

    (a) the day or the week or date on or in which,
    (b) the time at which,
    (c) the frequency with which, or
    (d) the locality or localities in which,

it is proposed to be conducted.

(2) In making a decision under subsection (1), a local authority may have regard to the fact (where it is the case) that the collection is proposed to be conducted—

    (a) wholly or partly in a locality in which another collection in a public place is already authorised to be conducted under this Chapter, and
    (b) on a day on which that other collection is already so authorised, or on the day falling immediately before, or immediately after, any such day.

(3) A local authority must not, however, have regard to the matters mentioned in subsection (2) if it appears to them—

    (a) that the proposed collection would be conducted only in one location, which is on land to which members of the public would have access only—

(i) by virtue of the express or implied permission of the occupier of the land, or
(ii) by virtue of any enactment, and

    (b) that the occupier of the land consents to that collection being conducted there;

and for this purpose "the occupier", in relation to unoccupied land, means the person entitled to occupy it.

(4) In this section a reference to a collection in a public place authorised under this Chapter is a reference to a collection in a public place that—

    (a) is conducted in accordance with section 48, or
    (b) is an exempt collection by virtue of section 50.

61. Withdrawal or variation etc. of permits

(1) Where subsection (2), (3) or (4) applies, a local authority who have issued a permit under section 59 may—

    (a) withdraw the permit,
    (b) attach any condition (or further condition) to the permit, or
    (c) vary any existing condition of the permit.

(2) This subsection applies where the local authority—

    (a) have reason to believe that there has been a change in the circumstances which prevailed at the time when they issued the permit, and
    (b) are of the opinion that, if the application for the permit had been made in the new circumstances, they would not have issued the permit or would have issued it subject to different or additional conditions.

(3) This subsection applies where the local authority have reason to believe that any information provided to them by the holder of a permit (or, where there is more than one holder, by any of them) for the purposes of the application for the permit was false or misleading in a material particular.

(4) This subsection applies where the local authority have reason to believe that there has been or is likely to be a breach of any condition of a permit issued by them, or that a breach of such a condition is continuing.

(5) Any condition imposed at any time by a local authority under subsection (1) (whether by attaching a new condition to the permit or by varying an existing condition) must be one that it would be appropriate for the authority to attach to the permit under section 59. (3) if the holder was applying for it in the circumstances prevailing at that time.

(6) The exercise by a local authority of the power conferred by paragraph (b) or (c) of subsection

(1) on one occasion does not prevent them from exercising any of the powers conferred by that subsection on a subsequent occasion; and on any subsequent occasion the reference in subsection (2)(a) to the time when the local authority issued the permit is a reference to the time when they last exercised any of those powers.

(7) Where under this section a local authority—
   (a) withdraw a permit,
   (b) attach a condition to a permit, or
   (c) vary an existing condition of a permit,
they must serve on the holder written notice of their decision and the reasons for their decision.

(8) That notice must also state the right of appeal conferred by section 62. (3) and the time within which such an appeal must be brought.

(9) Where a local authority withdraw a permit under this section, they must send a copy of their decision and the reasons for it to the Commission.

(10) Where a local authority under this section withdraw a permit, attach any condition to a permit, or vary an existing condition of a permit, the permit shall continue to have effect as if it had not been withdrawn or (as the case may be) as if the condition had not been attached or varied—
   (a) until the time for bringing an appeal under section 62. (3) has expired, or
   (b) if such an appeal is duly brought, until the determination or abandonment of the appeal.

62. Appeals against decisions of local authority

(1) A person who, in relation to a public charitable collection, has duly notified a local authority of the matters mentioned in section 50. (3) may appeal to a magistrates' court against a decision of the local authority under section 50. (4)—
   (a) that the collection is not a local, short-term collection, or
   (b) that the promoters or any of them has breached any such provision, or been convicted of any such offence, as is mentioned in paragraph (b) of that subsection.

(2) A person who has duly applied to a local authority for a permit to conduct a collection in a public place in the authority's area may appeal to a magistrates' court against a decision of the authority under section 59—
   (a) to refuse to issue a permit, or
   (b) to attach any condition to it.

(3) A person to whom a permit has been issued may appeal to a magistrates' court against a decision of the local authority under section 61—
   (a) to withdraw the permit,
   (b) to attach a condition to the permit, or
   (c) to vary an existing condition of the permit.

(4) An appeal under subsection (1), (2) or (3) shall be by way of complaint for an order, and the Magistrates' Courts Act 1980 (c. 43) shall apply to the proceedings.

(5) Any such appeal shall be brought within 14 days of the date of service on the person in question of the relevant notice under section 50. (4), section 59. (5) or (as the case may be) section 61. (7); and for the purposes of this section an appeal shall be taken to be brought when the complaint is made.

(6) An appeal against the decision of a magistrates' court on an appeal under subsection (1), (2) or (3) may be brought to the Crown Court.

(7) On an appeal to a magistrates' court or the Crown Court under this section, the court may confirm, vary or reverse the local authority's decision and generally give such directions as it thinks fit, having regard to the provisions of this Chapter and of any regulations under section 63.

(8) On an appeal against a decision of a local authority under section 50. (4), directions under subsection (7) may include a direction that the collection may be conducted—
   (a) on the date or dates notified in accordance with section 50. (3)(b), or
   (b) on such other date or dates as may be specified in the direction;
and if so conducted the collection is to be regarded as one that is an exempt collection by virtue of section 50.

(9) It shall be the duty of the local authority to comply with any directions given by the court under subsection (7); but the authority need not comply with any directions given by a magistrates' court—

(a) until the time for bringing an appeal under subsection (6) has expired, or

(b) if such an appeal is duly brought, until the determination or abandonment of the appeal.

Prospective

Supplementary

63. Regulations

(1) The [F4. Secretary of State] may make regulations—

(a) prescribing the matters which a local authority are to take into account in determining whether a collection is local in character for the purposes of section 50. (2)(a);

(b) for the purpose of regulating the conduct of public charitable collections;

(c) prescribing anything falling to be prescribed by virtue of any provision of this Chapter.

(2) The matters which may be prescribed by regulations under subsection (1)(a) include—

(a) the extent of the area within which the appeal is to be conducted;

(b) whether the appeal forms part of a series of appeals;

(c) the number of collectors making the appeal and whether they are acting for remuneration or otherwise;

(d) the financial resources (of any description) of any charitable, benevolent or philanthropic institution for whose benefit the appeal is to be conducted;

(e) where the promoters live or have any place of business.

(3) Regulations under subsection (1)(b) may make provision—

(a) about the keeping and publication of accounts;

(b) for the prevention of annoyance to members of the public;

(c) with respect to the use by collectors of badges and certificates of authority, or badges incorporating such certificates, including, in particular, provision—

(i) prescribing the form of such badges and certificates;

(ii) requiring a collector, on request, to permit his badge, or any certificate of authority held by him of the purposes of the collection, to be inspected by a constable or a duly authorised officer of a local authority, or by an occupier of any premises visited by him in the course of the collection;

(d) for prohibiting persons under a prescribed age from acting as collectors, and prohibiting others from causing them so to act.

(4) Nothing in subsection (2) or (3) prejudices the generality of subsection (1)(a) or (b).

(5) Regulations under this section may provide that any failure to comply with a specified provision of the regulations is to be an offence punishable on summary conviction by a fine not exceeding level 2 on the standard scale.

(6) Before making regulations under this section the[F5. Secretary of State] must consult such persons or bodies of persons as he considers appropriate.

Amendments (Textual)

F4. Words in s. 63. (1) substituted (9.11.2016) by The Transfer of Functions (Elections, Referendums, Third Sector and Information) Order 2016 (S.I. 2016/997), art. 1. (2), Sch. 2 para. 19. (2)(a) (with art. 12)

F5. Words in s. 63. (6) substituted (9.11.2016) by The Transfer of Functions (Elections, Referendums, Third Sector and Information) Order 2016 (S.I. 2016/997), art. 1. (2), Sch. 2 para. 19. (2)(a) (with art. 12)

Modifications etc. (not altering text)

C2. S. 63 functions transferred (9.11.2016) by The Transfer of Functions (Elections, Referendums, Third Sector and Information) Order 2016 (S.I. 2016/997), arts. 1. (2), 10. (2)(e) (with arts. 10. (3), 11, 12)

64. Offences

(1) A person commits an offence if, in connection with any charitable appeal, he displays or uses—

(a) a prescribed badge or prescribed certificate of authority which is not for the time being held by him for the purposes of the appeal pursuant to regulations under section 63, or

(b) any badge or article, or any certificate or other document, so nearly resembling a prescribed badge or (as the case may be) a prescribed certificate of authority as to be likely to deceive a member of the public.

(2) A person commits an offence if—

(a) for the purposes of an application made under section 51 or section 58, or

(b) for the purposes of section 49 or section 50,

he knowingly or recklessly furnishes any information which is false or misleading in a material particular.

(3) A person guilty of an offence under this section is liable on summary conviction to a fine not exceeding level 5 on the standard scale.

(4) In subsection (1) "prescribed badge" and "prescribed certificate of authority" mean respectively a badge and a certificate of authority in such form as may be prescribed.

65. Offences by bodies corporate

(1) Where any offence under this Chapter or any regulations made under it—

(a) is committed by a body corporate, and

(b) is proved to have been committed with the consent or connivance of, or to be attributable to any neglect on the part of, any director, manager, secretary or other similar officer of the body corporate, or any person who was purporting to act in any such capacity,

he as well as the body corporate shall be guilty of that offence and shall be liable to be proceeded against and punished accordingly.

(2) In subsection (1) "director", in relation to a body corporate whose affairs are managed by its members, means a member of the body corporate.

66. Service of documents

(1) This section applies to any notice required to be served under this Chapter.

(2) A notice to which this section applies may be served on a person (other than a body corporate)—

(a) by delivering it to that person;

(b) by leaving it at his last known address in the United Kingdom; or

(c) by sending it by post to him at that address.

(3) A notice to which this section applies may be served on a body corporate by delivering it or sending it by post—

(a) to the registered or principal office of the body in the United Kingdom, or

(b) if it has no such office in the United Kingdom, to any place in the United Kingdom where it carries on business or conducts its activities (as the case may be).

(4) A notice to which this section applies may also be served on a person (including a body corporate) by sending it by post to that person at an address notified by that person for the purposes of this subsection to the person or persons by whom it is required to be served.

Chapter 2. Fund-raising

67. Statements indicating benefits for charitable institutions and fund-raisers

(1) Section 60 of the Charities Act 1992 (c. 41) (fund-raisers required to indicate institutions benefiting and arrangements for remuneration) is amended as follows.

(2) In subsection (1) (statements by professional fund-raisers raising money for particular

charitable institutions), for paragraph (c) substitute—

"(c)the method by which the fund-raiser's remuneration in connection with the appeal is to be determined and the notifiable amount of that remuneration."

(3) In subsection (2) (statements by professional fund-raisers raising money for charitable purposes etc.), for paragraph (c) substitute—

"(c)the method by which his remuneration in connection with the appeal is to be determined and the notifiable amount of that remuneration."

(4) In subsection (3) (statements by commercial participators raising money for particular charitable institutions), for paragraph (c) substitute—

"(c)the notifiable amount of whichever of the following sums is applicable in the circumstances—

(i) the sum representing so much of the consideration given for goods or services sold or supplied by him as is to be given to or applied for the benefit of the institution or institutions concerned,

(ii) the sum representing so much of any other proceeds of a promotional venture undertaken by him as is to be so given or applied, or

(iii) the sum of the donations by him in connection with the sale or supply of any such goods or services which are to be so given or supplied."

(5) After subsection (3) insert—

"(3. A)In subsections (1) to (3) a reference to the "notifiable amount" of any remuneration or other sum is a reference—

(a) to the actual amount of the remuneration or sum, if that is known at the time when the statement is made; and

(b) otherwise to the estimated amount of the remuneration or sum, calculated as accurately as is reasonably possible in the circumstances."

Commencement Information

I4. S. 67 in force at 1.4.2008 by S.I. 2007/3286, art. 3, Sch. 2 (with art. 4)

68. Statements indicating benefits for charitable institutions and collectors

After section 60 of the 1992 Act insert—

"60. AOther persons making appeals required to indicate institutions benefiting and arrangements for remuneration

(1) Subsections (1) and (2) of section 60 apply to a person acting for reward as a collector in respect of a public charitable collection as they apply to a professional fund-raiser.

(2) But those subsections do not so apply to a person excluded by virtue of—

(a) subsection (3) below, or

(b) section 60. B(1) (exclusion of lower-paid collectors).

(3) Those subsections do not so apply to a person if—

(a) section 60. (1) or (2) applies apart from subsection (1) (by virtue of the exception in section 58. (2)(c) for persons treated as promoters), or

(b) subsection (4) or (5) applies,

in relation to his acting for reward as a collector in respect of the collection mentioned in subsection (1) above.

(4) Where a person within subsection (6) solicits money or other property for the benefit of one or more particular charitable institutions, the solicitation shall be accompanied by a statement clearly indicating—

(a) the name or names of the institution or institutions for whose benefit the solicitation is being made;

(b) if there is more than one such institution, the proportions in which the institutions are respectively to benefit;

(c) the fact that he is an officer, employee or trustee of the institution or company mentioned in subsection (6); and

(d) the fact that he is receiving remuneration as an officer, employee or trustee or (as the case may be) for acting as a collector.

(5) Where a person within subsection (6) solicits money or other property for charitable, benevolent or philanthropic purposes of any description (rather than for the benefit of one or more particular charitable institutions), the solicitation shall be accompanied by a statement clearly indicating—

(a) the fact that he is soliciting money or other property for those purposes and not for the benefit of any particular charitable institution or institutions;

(b) the method by which it is to be determined how the proceeds of the appeal are to be distributed between different charitable institutions;

(c) the fact that he is an officer, employee or trustee of the institution or company mentioned in subsection (6); and

(d) the fact that he is receiving remuneration as an officer, employee or trustee or (as the case may be) for acting as a collector.

(6) A person is within this subsection if—

(a) he is an officer or employee of a charitable institution or a company connected with any such institution, or a trustee of any such institution,

(b) he is acting as a collector in that capacity, and

(c) he receives remuneration either in his capacity as officer, employee or trustee or for acting as a collector.

(7) But a person is not within subsection (6) if he is excluded by virtue of section 60. B(4).

(8) Where any requirement of—

(a) subsection (1) or (2) of section 60, as it applies by virtue of subsection (1) above, or

(b) subsection (4) or (5) above,

is not complied with in relation to any solicitation, the collector concerned shall be guilty of an offence and liable on summary conviction to a fine not exceeding level 5 on the standard scale.

(9) Section 60. (8) and (9) apply in relation to an offence under subsection (8) above as they apply in relation to an offence under section 60. (7).

(10) In this section—

"the appeal", in relation to any solicitation by a collector, means the campaign or other fund-raising venture in the course of which the solicitation is made;

"collector" has the meaning given by section 47. (1) of the Charities Act 2006;

"public charitable collection" has the meaning given by section 45 of that Act.

60. BExclusion of lower-paid collectors from provisions of section 60. A

(1) Section 60. (1) and (2) do not apply (by virtue of section 60. A(1)) to a person who is under the earnings limit in subsection (2) below.

(2) A person is under the earnings limit in this subsection if he does not receive—

(a) more than—

(i) £5 per day, or

(ii) £500 per year,

by way of remuneration for acting as a collector in relation to relevant collections, or

(b) more than £500 by way of remuneration for acting as a collector in relation to the collection mentioned in section 60. A(1).

(3) In subsection (2) "relevant collections" means public charitable collections conducted for the benefit of—

(a) the charitable institution or institutions, or

(b) the charitable, benevolent or philanthropic purposes,

for whose benefit the collection mentioned in section 60. A(1) is conducted.

(4) A person is not within section 60. A(6) if he is under the earnings limit in subsection (5) below.

(5) A person is under the earnings limit in this subsection if the remuneration received by him as mentioned in section 60. A(6)(c)—

(a) is not more than—
(i) £5 per day, or
(ii) £500 per year, or
(b) if a lump sum, is not more than £500.
(6) The Minister may by order amend subsections (2) and (5) by substituting a different sum for any sum for the time being specified there."
Commencement Information
I5. S. 68 in force at 27.2.2007 for specified purposes by S.I. 2007/309, art. 2, Sch.
I6. S. 68 in force at 1.4.2008 for specified purposes by S.I. 2007/3286, art. 3, Sch. 2 (with art. 4)

69. Reserve power to control fund-raising by charitable institutions

After section 64 of the 1992 Act insert—
"64. AReserve power to control fund-raising by charitable institutions
(1) The Minister may make such regulations as appear to him to be necessary or desirable for or in connection with regulating charity fund-raising.
(2) In this section "charity fund-raising" means activities which are carried on by—
    (a) charitable institutions,
    (b) persons managing charitable institutions, or
    (c) persons or companies connected with such institutions,
and involve soliciting or otherwise procuring funds for the benefit of such institutions or companies connected with them, or for general charitable, benevolent or philanthropic purposes. But "activities" does not include primary purpose trading.
(3) Regulations under this section may, in particular, impose a good practice requirement on the persons managing charitable institutions in circumstances where—
    (a) those institutions,
    (b) the persons managing them, or
    (c) persons or companies connected with such institutions,
are engaged in charity fund-raising.
(4) A "good practice requirement" is a requirement to take all reasonable steps to ensure that the fund-raising is carried out in such a way that—
    (a) it does not unreasonably intrude on the privacy of those from whom funds are being solicited or procured;
    (b) it does not involve the making of unreasonably persistent approaches to persons to donate funds;
    (c) it does not result in undue pressure being placed on persons to donate funds;
    (d) it does not involve the making of any false or misleading representation about any of the matters mentioned in subsection (5).
(5) The matters are—
    (a) the extent or urgency of any need for funds on the part of any charitable institution or company connected with such an institution;
    (b) any use to which funds donated in response to the fund-raising are to be put by such an institution or company;
    (c) the activities, achievements or finances of such an institution or company.
(6) Regulations under this section may provide that a person who persistently fails, without reasonable excuse, to comply with any specified requirement of the regulations is to be guilty of an offence and liable on summary conviction to a fine not exceeding level 2 on the standard scale.
(7) For the purposes of this section—
    (a) "funds" means money or other property;
    (b) "general charitable, benevolent or philanthropic purposes" means charitable, benevolent or philanthropic purposes other than those associated with one or more particular institutions;

(c) the persons "managing" a charitable institution are the charity trustees or other persons having the general control and management of the administration of the institution; and
(d) a person is "connected" with a charitable institution if he is an employee or agent of—
(i) the institution,
(ii) the persons managing it, or
(iii) a company connected with it,
or he is a volunteer acting on behalf of the institution or such a company.
(8) In this section "primary purpose trading", in relation to a charitable institution, means any trade carried on by the institution or a company connected with it where—
(a) the trade is carried on in the course of the actual carrying out of a primary purpose of the institution; or
(b) the work in connection with the trade is mainly carried out by beneficiaries of the institution."
Commencement Information
I7. S. 69 in force at 27.2.2007 by S.I. 2007/309, art. 2, Sch.

Chapter 3. Financial assistance

70. Power of relevant Minister to give financial assistance to charitable, benevolent or philanthropic institutions

(1) A relevant Minister may give financial assistance to any charitable, benevolent or philanthropic institution in respect of any of the institution's activities which directly or indirectly benefit the whole or any part of England (whether or not they also benefit any other area).
(2) Financial assistance under subsection (1) may be given in any form and, in particular, may be given by way of—
 (a) grants,
 (b) loans,
 (c) guarantees, or
 (d) incurring expenditure for the benefit of the person assisted.
(3) Financial assistance under subsection (1) may be given on such terms and conditions as the relevant Minister considers appropriate.
(4) Those terms and conditions may, in particular, include provision as to—
 (a) the purposes for which the assistance may be used;
 (b) circumstances in which the assistance is to be repaid, or otherwise made good, to the relevant Minister, and the manner in which that is to be done;
 (c) the making of reports to the relevant Minister regarding the uses to which the assistance has been put;
 (d) the keeping, and making available for inspection, of accounts and other records;
 (e) the carrying out of examinations by the Comptroller and Auditor General into the economy, efficiency and effectiveness with which the assistance has been used;
 (f) the giving by the institution of financial assistance in any form to other persons on such terms and conditions as the institution or the relevant Minister considers appropriate.
(5) A person receiving assistance under this section must comply with the terms and conditions on which it is given, and compliance may be enforced by the relevant Minister.
(6) A relevant Minister may make arrangements for—
 (a) assistance under subsection (1) to be given, or
 (b) any other of his functions under this section to be exercised,
by some other person.
(7) Arrangements under subsection (6) may make provision for the functions concerned to be so

exercised—
- (a) either wholly or to such extent as may be specified in the arrangements, and
- (b) either generally or in such cases or circumstances as may be so specified,

but do not prevent the functions concerned from being exercised by a relevant Minister.

(8) As soon as possible after 31st March in each year, a relevant Minister must make a report on any exercise by him of any powers under this section during the period of 12 months ending on that day.

(9) The relevant Minister must lay a copy of the report before each House of Parliament.

(10) In this section "charitable, benevolent or philanthropic institution" means—
- (a) a charity, or
- (b) an institution (other than a charity) which is established for charitable, benevolent or philanthropic purposes.

(11) In this section "relevant Minister" means the Secretary of State [F6or the Minister for the Cabinet Office].

Amendments (Textual)
F6. Words in s. 70. (11) substituted (18.8.2010) by Transfer of Functions (Equality) Order 2010 (S.I. 2010/1839), art. 1. (2), Sch. para. 8
Modifications etc. (not altering text)
C3. S. 70 functions made exercisable concurrently (12.10.2007) by Transfer of Functions (Equality) Order 2007 (S.I. 2007/2914), arts. 1. (2), 3. (4)(b)
C4. S. 70 functions ceased to be exercisable concurrently (18.8.2010) by Transfer of Functions (Equality) Order 2010 (S.I. 2010/1839), arts. 1. (2), 3. (2)(b)
Commencement Information
I8. S. 70 in force at 1.4.2007 by S.I. 2007/309, art. 3

71. Power of National Assembly for Wales to give financial assistance to charitable, benevolent or philanthropic institutions

(1) The National Assembly for Wales may give financial assistance to any charitable, benevolent or philanthropic institution in respect of any of the institution's activities which directly or indirectly benefit the whole or any part of Wales (whether or not they also benefit any other area).

(2) Financial assistance under subsection (1) may be given in any form and, in particular, may be given by way of—
- (a) grants,
- (b) loans,
- (c) guarantees, or
- (d) incurring expenditure for the benefit of the person assisted.

(3) Financial assistance under subsection (1) may be given on such terms and conditions as the Assembly considers appropriate.

(4) Those terms and conditions may, in particular, include provision as to—
- (a) the purposes for which the assistance may be used;
- (b) circumstances in which the assistance is to be repaid, or otherwise made good, to the Assembly, and the manner in which that is to be done;
- (c) the making of reports to the Assembly regarding the uses to which the assistance has been put;
- (d) the keeping, and making available for inspection, of accounts and other records;
- (e) the carrying out of examinations by the Auditor General for Wales into the economy, efficiency and effectiveness with which the assistance has been used;
- (f) the giving by the institution of financial assistance in any form to other persons on such terms and conditions as the institution or the Assembly considers appropriate.

(5) A person receiving assistance under this section must comply with the terms and conditions on which it is given, and compliance may be enforced by the Assembly.

(6) The Assembly may make arrangements for—
 (a) assistance under subsection (1) to be given, or
 (b) any other of its functions under this section to be exercised,
by some other person.
(7) Arrangements under subsection (6) may make provision for the functions concerned to be so exercised—
 (a) either wholly or to such extent as may be specified in the arrangements, and
 (b) either generally or in such cases or circumstances as may be so specified,
but do not prevent the functions concerned from being exercised by the Assembly.
(8) After 31st March in each year, the Assembly must publish a report on the exercise of powers under this section during the period of 12 months ending on that day.
(9) In this section "charitable, benevolent or philanthropic institution" means—
 (a) a charity, or
 (b) an institution (other than a charity) which is established for charitable, benevolent or philanthropic purposes.
Commencement Information
I9. S. 71 in force at 27.2.2007 by S.I. 2007/309, art. 2, Sch.

Part 4. Miscellaneous and general

Part 4 Miscellaneous and general

72. Disclosure of information to and by Northern Ireland regulator

(1) This section applies if a body (referred to in this section as "the Northern Ireland regulator") is established to exercise functions in Northern Ireland which are similar in nature to the functions exercised in England and Wales by the Charity Commission.
(2) The [F1. Secretary of State] may by regulations authorise relevant public authorities to disclose information to the Northern Ireland regulator for the purpose of enabling or assisting the Northern Ireland regulator to discharge any of its functions.
(3) If the regulations authorise the disclosure of Revenue and Customs information, they must contain provision in relation to that disclosure which corresponds to the provision made in relation to the disclosure of such information by [F2section 55 of the Charities Act 2011] F3....
(4) In the case of information disclosed to the Northern Ireland regulator pursuant to regulations made under this section, any power of the Northern Ireland regulator to disclose the information is exercisable subject to any express restriction subject to which the information was disclosed to the Northern Ireland regulator.
(5) Subsection (4) does not apply in relation to Revenue and Customs information disclosed to the Northern Ireland regulator pursuant to regulations made under this section; but any such information may not be further disclosed except with the consent of the Commissioners for Her Majesty's Revenue and Customs.
(6) Any person specified, or of a description specified, in regulations made under this section who discloses information in contravention of subsection (5) is guilty of an offence and liable—
 (a) on summary conviction, to imprisonment for a term not exceeding 12 months or to a fine not exceeding the statutory maximum, or both;
 (b) on conviction on indictment, to imprisonment for a term not exceeding two years or to a fine, or both.
(7) It is a defence for a person charged with an offence under subsection (5) of disclosing

information to prove that he reasonably believed—
   (a) that the disclosure was lawful, or
   (b) that the information had already and lawfully been made available to the public.
(8) In the application of this section to Scotland or Northern Ireland, the reference to 12 months in subsection (6) is to be read as a reference to 6 months.
(9) In this section—
"relevant public authority" means—
   - any government department (other than a Northern Ireland department),
   - any local authority in England, Wales or Scotland,
   - any person who is a constable in England and Wales or Scotland,
   - any other body or person discharging functions of a public nature (including a body or person discharging regulatory functions in relation to any description of activities), except a body or person whose functions are exercisable only or mainly in or as regards Northern Ireland and relate only or mainly to transferred matters;
"Revenue and Customs information" means information held as mentioned in section 18. (1) of the Commissioners for Revenue and Customs Act 2005 (c. 11);
"transferred matter" has the same meaning as in the Northern Ireland Act 1998 (c. 47).
Amendments (Textual)
F1. Words in s. 72. (2) substituted (9.11.2016) by The Transfer of Functions (Elections, Referendums, Third Sector and Information) Order 2016 (S.I. 2016/997), art. 1. (2), Sch. 2 para. 19. (2)(b) (with art. 12)
F2. Words in s. 72. (3) substituted (14.3.2012) by Charities Act 2011 (c. 25), s. 355, Sch. 7 para. 119 (with s. 20. (2), Sch. 8)
F3. Words in s. 72. (3) repealed (with effect in accordance with s. 1184. (1) of the commencing Act) by Corporation Tax Act 2010 (c. 4), s. 1184. (1), Sch. 1 para. 493, Sch. 3 Pt. 1 (with Sch. 2)
Modifications etc. (not altering text)
C1. S. 72 functions transferred (9.11.2016) by The Transfer of Functions (Elections, Referendums, Third Sector and Information) Order 2016 (S.I. 2016/997), arts. 1. (2), 10. (2)(e) (with arts. 10. (3), 11, 12)
Commencement Information
I1. S. 72 in force at 27.2.2007 by S.I. 2007/309, art. 2, Sch.

73. Report on operation of this Act

(1) The [F4. Secretary of State] must, before the end of the period of five years beginning with the day on which this Act is passed, appoint a person to review generally the operation of this Act.
(2) The review must address, in particular, the following matters—
   (a) the effect of the Act on—
(i) excepted charities,
(ii) public confidence in charities,
(iii) the level of charitable donations, and
(iv) the willingness of individuals to volunteer,
   (b) the status of the Charity Commission as a government department, and
   (c) any other matters the Minister considers appropriate.
(3) After the person appointed under subsection (1) has completed his review, he must compile a report of his conclusions.
(4) The [F5. Secretary of State] must lay before Parliament a copy of the report mentioned in subsection (3).
(5) For the purposes of this section a charity is an excepted charity if—
   (a) it falls within paragraph (b) or (c) of section 3. A(2) of the 1993 Act (as amended by section 9 of this Act), or
   (b) it does not fall within either of those paragraphs but, immediately before [F631 January

2009], it fell within section 3. (5)(b) or (5. B)(b) of the 1993 Act.

[F7. (6)This section has effect, in relation to any time occurring on or after the commencement of the Charities Act 2011 as if—

(a) the reference in subsection (1) to the operation of this Act included (in relation to provisions of this Act repealed and re-enacted by the 2011 Act) a reference to the operation of the 2011 Act,

(b) the reference in subsection (2)(a) to the effect of the Act included (in relation to provisions of this Act repealed and re-enacted by the 2011 Act) a reference to the effect of the 2011 Act, and

(c) the reference in subsection (5)(a) to paragraph (b) or (c) of section 3. A(2) of the 1993 Act (as amended by section 9 of this Act) were a reference to paragraph (b) or (c) of section 30. (2) of the 2011 Act.]

Amendments (Textual)

F4. Words in s. 73. (1) substituted (9.11.2016) by The Transfer of Functions (Elections, Referendums, Third Sector and Information) Order 2016 (S.I. 2016/997), art. 1. (2), Sch. 2 para. 19. (2)(c) (with art. 12)

F5. Words in s. 73. (4) substituted (9.11.2016) by The Transfer of Functions (Elections, Referendums, Third Sector and Information) Order 2016 (S.I. 2016/997), art. 1. (2), Sch. 2 para. 19. (2)(c) (with art. 12)

F6. Words in s. 73. (5)(b) substituted (14.3.2012) by Charities Act 2011 (c. 25), s. 355, Sch. 7 para. 120. (1) (with s. 20. (2), Sch. 8)

F7. S. 73. (6) inserted (14.3.2012) by Charities Act 2011 (c. 25), s. 355, Sch. 7 para. 120. (2) (with s. 20. (2), Sch. 8)

Modifications etc. (not altering text)

C2. S. 73 functions transferred (9.11.2016) by The Transfer of Functions (Elections, Referendums, Third Sector and Information) Order 2016 (S.I. 2016/997), arts. 1. (2), 10. (2)(e) (with arts. 10. (3), 11, 12)

Commencement Information

I2. S. 73 in force at 31.1.2009 by S.I. 2008/3267, art. 2, Sch. (with arts. 3-27) (as amended: (29.9.2009) by S.I. 2009/2648, art. 3; (26.7.2010) by S.I. 2010/1942, art. 2; and (1.8.2011) by S.I. 2011/1725, arts. 1. (2), 3, Sch. para. 6)

General

74. Orders and regulations

(1) Any power of a relevant Minister to make an order or regulations under this Act is exercisable by statutory instrument.

(2) Any such power—

(a) may be exercised so as to make different provision for different cases or descriptions of case or different purposes or areas, and

(b) includes power to make such incidental, supplementary, consequential, transitory, transitional or saving provision as the relevant Minister considers appropriate.

(3) Subject to subsection (4), orders or regulations made by a relevant Minister under this Act are to be subject to annulment in pursuance of a resolution of either House of Parliament.

(4) Subsection (3) does not apply to—

F8. (a). . . . .

F8. (b). . . . .

(c) any regulations under section 72,

(d) any order under section 75. (4) which amends or repeals any provision of an Act or an Act of the Scottish Parliament,

(e) any order under section F9... 77, or

(f) any order under section 79. (2).

(5) No order or regulations within subsection (4) F10... (c), (d) or (e) may be made by a relevant Minister (whether alone or with other provisions) unless a draft of the order or regulations has been laid before, and approved by resolution of, each House of Parliament.
F11. (6). . . . .
(7) In this section "relevant Minister" means the Secretary of State or the Minister for the Cabinet Office.

Amendments (Textual)
F8. S. 74. (4)(a)(b) repealed (14.3.2012) by Charities Act 2011 (c. 25), s. 355, Sch. 7 para. 121. (1)(a), Sch. 10 (with s. 20. (2), Sch. 8)
F9. Words in s. 74. (4)(e) repealed (14.3.2012) by Charities Act 2011 (c. 25), s. 355, Sch. 7 para. 121. (1)(b), Sch. 10 (with s. 20. (2), Sch. 8)
F10. Words in s. 74. (5) repealed (14.3.2012) by Charities Act 2011 (c. 25), s. 355, Sch. 7 para. 121. (2), Sch. 10 (with s. 20. (2), Sch. 8)
F11. S. 74. (6) repealed (14.3.2012) by Charities Act 2011 (c. 25), s. 355, Sch. 7 para. 121. (3), Sch. 10 (with s. 20. (2), Sch. 8)

75. Amendments, repeals, revocations and transitional provisions

(1) Schedule 8 contains minor and consequential amendments.
(2) Schedule 9 makes provision for the repeal and revocation of enactments (including enactments which are spent).
(3) Schedule 10 contains transitional provisions and savings.
(4) A relevant Minister may by order make—
    (a) such supplementary, incidental or consequential provision, or
    (b) such transitory, transitional or saving provision,
as he considers appropriate for the general purposes, or any particular purposes, of this Act or in consequence of, or for giving full effect to, any provision made by this Act.
(5) An order under subsection (4) may amend, repeal, revoke or otherwise modify any enactment (including an enactment restating, with or without modifications, an enactment amended by this Act).
(6) In this section "relevant Minister" means the Secretary of State or the Minister for the Cabinet Office.

Commencement Information
I3. S. 75 partly in force; s. 75. (1) in force at Royal Assent for certain purposes, see s. 79. (1)(g); s. 75. (4)(5) in force at Royal Assent, see s. 79. (1)(c)
I4. S. 75. (1)-(3) in force at 27.2.2007 for specified purposes by S.I. 2007/309, art. 2, Sch.
I5. S. 75. (1)-(3) in force at 18.3.2008 for specified purposes by S.I. 2008/751, art. 2, Sch.
I6. S. 75. (1)-(3) in force at 1.4.2008 for specified purposes by S.I. 2008/945, art. 2, Sch. 1 (with arts. 4, 5)
I7. S. 75. (1)(3) in force at 1.4.2008 for specified purposes by S.I. 2007/3286, art. 3, Sch. 2 (with art. 4)
I8. S. 75. (1)-(3) in force at 31.1.2009 for specified purposes by S.I. 2008/3267, art. 2, Sch. (with arts. 3-27) (as amended: (29.9.2009) by S.I. 2009/2648, art. 3; (26.7.2010) by S.I. 2010/1942, art. 2; and (1.8.2011) by S.I. 2011/1725, arts. 1. (2), 3, Sch. para. 6)
I9. S. 75. (1)(2) in force at 30.9.2009 for specified purposes by S.I. 2009/2648, art. 2. (2)(c)
I10. S. 75. (1)-(3) in force at 1.6.2010 for specified purposes by S.I. 2010/503, art. 2, Sch. 1 (with Sch. 2)
I11. S. 75. (1)-(3) in force at 1.8.2011 for specified purposes by S.I. 2011/1728, art. 2, Sch. 1 (with Sch. 2)
I12. S. 75. (2)(3) in force at 28.11.2007 for specified purposes by S.I. 2007/3286, art. 2, Sch. 1
I13. S. 75. (2)(3) in force at 1.4.2010 for specified purposes by S.I. 2008/945, art. 2. A, Sch. 1. A (as inserted (30.3.2009) by S.I. 2009/841, art. 2. (2)(6))

I14. S. 75. (6) in force at 27.2.2007 by S.I. 2007/309, art. 2, Sch.

F1276. Pre-consolidation amendments

. . . .
Amendments (Textual)
F12. S. 76 repealed (14.3.2012) by Charities Act 2011 (c. 25), s. 355, Sch. 7 para. 122, Sch. 10 (with s. 20. (2), Sch. 8)

77. Amendments reflecting changes in company law audit provisions

(1) The [F13. Secretary of State] may by order make such amendments of the 1993 Act or this Act as he considers appropriate—
　(a) in consequence of, or in connection with, any changes made or to be made by any enactment to the provisions of company law relating to the accounts of charitable companies or to the auditing of, or preparation of reports in respect of, such accounts;
　(b) for the purposes of, or in connection with, applying provisions of Schedule 5. A to the 1993 Act (group accounts) to charitable companies that are not required to produce group accounts under company law.
(2) In this section—
"accounts" includes group accounts;
"amendments" includes repeals and modifications;
"charitable companies" means companies which are charities;
"company law" means the enactments relating to companies.
Amendments (Textual)
F13. Words in s. 77 substituted (9.11.2016) by The Transfer of Functions (Elections, Referendums, Third Sector and Information) Order 2016 (S.I. 2016/997), art. 1. (2), Sch. 2 para. 19. (2)(d) (with art. 12)
Modifications etc. (not altering text)
C3. S. 77 functions transferred (9.11.2016) by The Transfer of Functions (Elections, Referendums, Third Sector and Information) Order 2016 (S.I. 2016/997), arts. 1. (2), 10. (2)(e) (with arts. 10. (3), 11, 12)

78. Interpretation

(1) In this Act—
"the 1992 Act" means the Charities Act 1992 (c. 41);
"the 1993 Act" means the Charities Act 1993 (c. 10).
(2) In this Act—
　F14. (a). . . . .
　(b) "charitable purposes" has [F15 (in accordance with section 2. (2) of the Charities Act 2011) the meaning given by section 2. (1) of that Act]; and
　(c) "charity trustees" has the same meaning as in [F16that Act];
F17...
F18. (3). . . . .
(4) In this Act "enactment" includes—
　(a) any provision of subordinate legislation (within the meaning of the Interpretation Act 1978 (c. 30)),
　(b) a provision of a Measure of the Church Assembly or of the General Synod of the Church of England, and

(c) (in the context of section F19... 75. (5)) any provision made by or under an Act of the Scottish Parliament or Northern Ireland legislation,
and references to enactments include enactments passed or made after the passing of this Act.
(5) In this Act "institution" means an institution whether incorporated or not, and includes a trust or undertaking.
F20. (6). . . . .
(7) Subsections (2) to (5) apply except where the context otherwise requires.
Amendments (Textual)
F14. S. 78. (2)(a) repealed (14.3.2012) by Charities Act 2011 (c. 25), s. 355, Sch. 7 para. 123. (1)(a), Sch. 10 (with s. 20. (2), Sch. 8)
F15. Words in s. 78. (2)(b) substituted (14.3.2012) by Charities Act 2011 (c. 25), s. 355, Sch. 7 para. 123. (1)(b), Sch. 10 (with s. 20. (2), Sch. 8)
F16. Words in s. 78. (2)(c) substituted (14.3.2012) by Charities Act 2011 (c. 25), s. 355, Sch. 7 para. 123. (1)(c) (with s. 20. (2), Sch. 8)
F17. Words in s. 78. (2) repealed (14.3.2012) by Charities Act 2011 (c. 25), s. 355, Sch. 7 para. 123. (1)(d), Sch. 10 (with s. 20. (2), Sch. 8)
F18. S. 78. (3) repealed (14.3.2012) by Charities Act 2011 (c. 25), s. 355, Sch. 7 para. 123. (2), Sch. 10 (with s. 20. (2), Sch. 8)
F19. Words in s. 78. (4)(c) repealed (14.3.2012) by Charities Act 2011 (c. 25), s. 355, Sch. 7 para. 123. (3), Sch. 10 (with s. 20. (2), Sch. 8)
F20. Words in s. 78. (6) omitted (9.11.2016) by virtue of The Transfer of Functions (Elections, Referendums, Third Sector and Information) Order 2016 (S.I. 2016/997), art. 1. (2), Sch. 2 para. 19. (3) (with art. 12)

79. Commencement

(1) The following provisions come into force on the day on which this Act is passed—
    F21. (a). . . . .
    (b) section 74,
    (c) section 75. (4) and (5),
    (d) section 78,
    (e) section 77,
    (f) this section and section 80, and
    (g) the following provisions of Schedule 8—
    - paragraph 90. (2),
    - F22...
and section 75. (1) so far as relating to those provisions.
(2) Otherwise, this Act comes into force on such day as the [F23. Secretary of State]may by order appoint.
(3) An order under subsection (2)—
    (a) may appoint different days for different purposes or different areas;
    (b) make such provision as the [F24. Secretary of State] considers necessary or expedient for transitory, transitional or saving purposes in connection with the coming into force of any provision of this Act.
Amendments (Textual)
F21. S. 79. (1)(a) repealed (14.3.2012) by Charities Act 2011 (c. 25), s. 355, Sch. 7 para. 124. (a), Sch. 10 (with s. 20. (2), Sch. 8)
F22. Words in s. 79. (1)(g) repealed (14.3.2012) by Charities Act 2011 (c. 25), s. 355, Sch. 7 para. 124. (b), Sch. 10 (with s. 20. (2), Sch. 8)
F23. Words in s. 79. (2) substituted (9.11.2016) by The Transfer of Functions (Elections, Referendums, Third Sector and Information) Order 2016 (S.I. 2016/997), art. 1. (2), Sch. 2 para. 19. (2)(e) (with art. 12)

F24. Words in s. 79. (3) substituted (9.11.2016) by The Transfer of Functions (Elections, Referendums, Third Sector and Information) Order 2016 (S.I. 2016/997), art. 1. (2), Sch. 2 para. 19. (2)(e) (with art. 12)
Modifications etc. (not altering text)
C4. S. 79 functions transferred (9.11.2016) by The Transfer of Functions (Elections, Referendums, Third Sector and Information) Order 2016 (S.I. 2016/997), arts. 1. (2), 10. (2)(e) (with arts. 10. (3), 11, 12)

80. Short title and extent

(1) This Act may be cited as the Charities Act 2006.
(2) Subject to subsections (3) to (7), this Act extends to England and Wales only.
(3) The following provisions extend also to Scotland—
　　F25. (a)............................
　　F25. (b)............................
　　(c) sections 72 and 74,
　　F25. (d)........................... and
　　(e) section 75. (4) and (5), sections [F2677] to 79 and this section.
F27. (4)...............................
(5) The following provisions extend also to Northern Ireland—
　　F28. (a)............................
　　F28. (b)............................
　　F28. (c)............................
　　(d) sections 72 and 74,
　　F28. (e)........................... and
　　(f) section 75. (4) and (5), sections [F2977] to 79 and this section.
F30. (6)...............................
(7) Any amendment, repeal or revocation made by this Act has the same extent as the enactment to which it relates.
F31. (8)...............................
(9) Subsection (7) F32... does not apply to—
　　F33. (a)............................
　　(b) [F34the amendments] made by Schedule 8 in the Police, Factories, &c. (Miscellaneous Provisions) Act 1916 (c. 31), or
　　(c) the repeal made in that Act by Schedule 9,
which extend to England and Wales only.
Amendments (Textual)
F25. S. 80. (3)(a)(b)(d) repealed (14.3.2012) by Charities Act 2011 (c. 25), s. 355, Sch. 7 para. 125. (a), Sch. 10 (with s. 20. (2), Sch. 8)
F26. Figure in s. 80. (3)(e) substituted (14.3.2012) by Charities Act 2011 (c. 25), s. 355, Sch. 7 para. 125. (b) (with s. 20. (2), Sch. 8)
F27. S. 80. (4) repealed (14.3.2012) by Charities Act 2011 (c. 25), s. 355, Sch. 7 para. 125. (a), Sch. 10 (with s. 20. (2), Sch. 8)
F28. S. 80. (5)(a)-(c)(e) repealed (14.3.2012) by Charities Act 2011 (c. 25), s. 355, Sch. 7 para. 125. (a), Sch. 10 (with s. 20. (2), Sch. 8)
F29. Figure in s. 80. (5)(f) substituted (14.3.2012) by Charities Act 2011 (c. 25), s. 355, Sch. 7 para. 125. (b) (with s. 20. (2), Sch. 8)
F30. S. 80. (6) repealed (14.3.2012) by Charities Act 2011 (c. 25), s. 355, Sch. 7 para. 125. (a), Sch. 10 (with s. 20. (2), Sch. 8)
F31. S. 80. (8) repealed (14.3.2012) by Charities Act 2011 (c. 25), s. 355, Sch. 7 para. 125. (a), Sch. 10 (with s. 20. (2), Sch. 8)
F32. Word in s. 80. (9) repealed (14.3.2012) by Charities Act 2011 (c. 25), s. 355, Sch. 7 para.

125. (c)(i), Sch. 10 (with s. 20. (2), Sch. 8)
F33. S. 80. (9)(a) repealed (14.3.2012) by Charities Act 2011 (c. 25), s. 355, Sch. 7 para. 125. (c)(i), Sch. 10 (with s. 20. (2), Sch. 8)
F34. Words in s. 80. (9)(b) substituted (14.3.2012) by Charities Act 2011 (c. 25), s. 355, Sch. 7 para. 125. (c)(ii), Sch. 10 (with s. 20. (2), Sch. 8)

Schedules

Schedule 1. The Charity Commission

Section 6
....
Amendments (Textual)
F1. Schs. 1, 2 repealed (14.3.2012) by Charities Act 2011 (c. 25), s. 355, Sch. 10 (with s. 20. (2), Sch. 8)

Schedule 2. Establishment of the Charity Commission: supplementary

Section 6
....
Amendments (Textual)
F1. Schs. 1, 2 repealed (14.3.2012) by Charities Act 2011 (c. 25), s. 355, Sch. 10 (with s. 20. (2), Sch. 8)

Schedule 3. The Charity Tribunal

Section 8
....
Amendments (Textual)
F1. Sch. 3 repealed (1.9.2009) by The Transfer of Functions of the Charity Tribunal Order 2009 (S.I. 2009/1834), art. 1, Sch. 3 (with Sch. 4)

Schedule 4. Appeals and applications to Charity Tribunal

Section 8

F1...
Amendments (Textual)

F1. Schs. 4-7 repealed (14.3.2012) by Charities Act 2011 (c. 25), s. 355, Sch. 10 (with s. 20. (2), Sch. 8)

Schedule 5. Exempt charities: increased regulation under 1993 Act

Section 12

F1...

Amendments (Textual)
F1. Schs. 4-7 repealed (14.3.2012) by Charities Act 2011 (c. 25), s. 355, Sch. 10 (with s. 20. (2), Sch. 8)

Schedule 6. Group accounts

Section 30

F1...
Amendments (Textual)
F1. Schs. 4-7 repealed (14.3.2012) by Charities Act 2011 (c. 25), s. 355, Sch. 10 (with s. 20. (2), Sch. 8)

Schedule 7. Charitable incorporated organisations

Section 34
....
Amendments (Textual)
F1. Schs. 4-7 repealed (14.3.2012) by Charities Act 2011 (c. 25), s. 355, Sch. 10 (with s. 20. (2), Sch. 8)

Schedule 8. Minor and consequential amendments

Section 75

Literary and Scientific Institutions Act 1854 (c. 112)

F11............................
Amendments (Textual)
F1. Sch. 8 paras. 1, 2 repealed (14.3.2012) by Charities Act 2011 (c. 25), s. 355, Sch. 10 (with s. 20. (2), Sch. 8)

Places of Worship Registration Act 1855 (c. 81)

F1 2. . . . .

Bishops Trusts Substitution Act 1858 (c. 71)

3. The Bishops Trusts Substitution Act 1858 has effect subject to the following amendments.
Commencement Information
I1. Sch. 8 para. 3 in force at 27.2.2007 by S.I. 2007/309, art. 2, Sch.
4. In section 1 (substitution of one bishop for another as trustee)—
(a) for "Charity Commissioners" substitute " Charity Commission ", and
(b) for "them" substitute " it ".
Commencement Information
I2. Sch. 8 para. 4 in force at 27.2.2007 by S.I. 2007/309, art. 2, Sch.
5. In section 3 (how costs are to be defrayed) for "said Charity Commissioners" (in both places) substitute " Charity Commission ".
Commencement Information
I3. Sch. 8 para. 5 in force at 27.2.2007 by S.I. 2007/309, art. 2, Sch.

Places of Worship Sites Amendment Act 1882 (c. 21)

F26. . . . .
Amendments (Textual)
F2. Sch. 8 para. 6 repealed (14.3.2012) by Charities Act 2011 (c. 25), s. 355, Sch. 10 (with s. 20.(2), Sch. 8)

Municipal Corporations Act 1882 (c. 50)

7. In section 133. (2) of the Municipal Corporations Act 1882 (administration of charitable trusts and vesting of legal estate) for "Charity Commissioners" substitute " Charity Commission ".
Commencement Information
I4. Sch. 8 para. 7 in force at 27.2.2007 by S.I. 2007/309, art. 2, Sch.

Technical and Industrial Institutions Act 1892 (c. 29)

F38. . . . .
Amendments (Textual)
F3. Sch. 8 para. 8 repealed (14.3.2012) by Charities Act 2011 (c. 25), s. 355, Sch. 10 (with s. 20.(2), Sch. 8)

Local Government Act 1894 (c. 73)

9. (1)In section 75. (2) of the Local Government Act 1894 (construction of that Act) the definition of "ecclesiastical charity" is amended as follows.
(2) In the second paragraph (proviso)—
(a) for "Charity Commissioners" substitute " Charity Commission ", and
(b) for "them" substitute " it ".
(3) In the third paragraph (inclusion of other buildings) for "Charity Commissioners" substitute " Charity Commission ".

Commencement Information
I5. Sch. 8 para. 9 in force at 27.2.2007 by S.I. 2007/309, art. 2, Sch.

Commons Act 1899 (c. 30)

10. In section 18 of the Commons Act 1899 (power to modify provisions as to recreation grounds)—
(a) for "Charity Commissioners" substitute " Charity Commission ", and
(b) for "their" substitute " its ".
Commencement Information
I6. Sch. 8 para. 10 in force at 27.2.2007 by S.I. 2007/309, art. 2, Sch.

Open Spaces Act 1906 (c. 25)

11. The Open Spaces Act 1906 has effect subject to the following amendments.
Commencement Information
I7. Sch. 8 para. 11 in force at 27.2.2007 by S.I. 2007/309, art. 2, Sch.
12. In section 3. (1) (transfer to local authority of spaces held by trustees for purposes of public recreation) for "Charity Commissioners" substitute " Charity Commission ".
Commencement Information
I8. Sch. 8 para. 12 in force at 27.2.2007 by S.I. 2007/309, art. 2, Sch.
13. (1)Section 4 (transfer by charity trustees of open space to local authority) is amended as follows.
(2) In subsection (1), for the words from "and with the sanction" to "as hereinafter provided" substitute " and in accordance with subsection (1. A) ".
(3) After subsection (1) insert—
"(1. A)The trustees act in accordance with this subsection if they convey or demise the open space as mentioned in subsection (1)—
    (a) with the sanction of an order of the Charity Commission or with that of an order of the court to be obtained as provided in the following provisions of this section, or
    (b) in accordance with such provisions of section 36. (2) to (8) of the Charities Act 1993 as are applicable."
F4. (4). . . . .
Amendments (Textual)
F4. Sch. 8 para. 13. (4) repealed (14.3.2012) by Charities Act 2011 (c. 25), s. 355, Sch. 10 (with s. 20. (2), Sch. 8)
Commencement Information
I9. Sch. 8 para. 13 in force at 27.2.2007 by S.I. 2007/309, art. 2, Sch.
14. In section 21. (1) (application to Ireland)—
(a) for "Charity Commissioners" substitute " Charity Commission ", and
(b) for "Commissioners of Charity Donations and Bequests for Ireland" substitute " the Department for Social Development ".
Commencement Information
I10. Sch. 8 para. 14 in force at 27.2.2007 by S.I. 2007/309, art. 2, Sch.
Prospective

Police, Factories, &c. (Miscellaneous Provisions) Act 1916 (c. 31)

15. (1)Section 5 of the Police, Factories, &c. (Miscellaneous Provisions) Act 1916 (regulation of street collections) is amended as follows.
(2) In subsection (1) for "the benefit of charitable or other purposes," substitute " any purposes in

circumstances not involving the making of a charitable appeal, ".
(3) In paragraph (b) of the proviso to subsection (1) omit the words from " , and no representation " onwards.
(4) In subsection (4) before the definition of "street" insert—
""charitable appeal" has the same meaning as in Chapter 1 of Part 3 of the Charities Act 2006;".

National Trust Charity Scheme Confirmation Act 1919 (c. lxxxiv)

16. The National Trust Charity Scheme Confirmation Act 1919 has effect subject to the following amendments.
Commencement Information
I11. Sch. 8 para. 16 in force at 27.2.2007 by S.I. 2007/309, art. 2, Sch.
17. In section 1 (confirmation of the scheme) for "Charity Commissioners" substitute " Charity Commission ".
Commencement Information
I12. Sch. 8 para. 17 in force at 27.2.2007 by S.I. 2007/309, art. 2, Sch.
18. In paragraph 3 of the scheme set out in the Schedule, for "Charity Commissioners upon such application made to them for the purpose as they think" substitute " Charity Commission upon such application made to it for the purpose as it thinks ".
Commencement Information
I13. Sch. 8 para. 18 in force at 27.2.2007 by S.I. 2007/309, art. 2, Sch.

Settled Land Act 1925 (c. 18)

19. In section 29. (3) of the Settled Land Act 1925 (charitable and public trusts: saving) for "Charity Commissioners" substitute " Charity Commission ".
Commencement Information
I14. Sch. 8 para. 19 in force at 27.2.2007 by S.I. 2007/309, art. 2, Sch.

Landlord and Tenant Act 1927 (c. 36)

20. In Part 2 of the Second Schedule to the Landlord and Tenant Act 1927 (application to ecclesiastical and charity land), in paragraph 2, for "Charity Commissioners" substitute " Charity Commission ".
Commencement Information
I15. Sch. 8 para. 20 in force at 27.2.2007 by S.I. 2007/309, art. 2, Sch.

Voluntary Hospitals (Paying Patients) Act 1936 (c. 17)

21. The Voluntary Hospitals (Paying Patients) Act 1936 has effect subject to the following amendments.
Commencement Information
I16. Sch. 8 para. 21 in force at 27.2.2007 by S.I. 2007/309, art. 2, Sch.
22. In section 1 (definitions), in the definition of "Order", for "Charity Commissioners" substitute " Charity Commission ".
Commencement Information
I17. Sch. 8 para. 22 in force at 27.2.2007 by S.I. 2007/309, art. 2, Sch.
23. (1)Section 2 (accommodation for and charges to paying patients) is amended as follows.
(2) In subsections (1), (3) and (4) for "Charity Commissioners" substitute " Charity Commission ".
(3) In subsection (4)—

(a) for "the Commissioners" (in both places) substitute " the Commission ",
(b) for "they" substitute " it ", and
(c) for "their" substitute " its ".
Commencement Information
I18. Sch. 8 para. 23 in force at 27.2.2007 by S.I. 2007/309, art. 2, Sch.
24. In section 3. (1) (provision for patients able to make some, but not full, payment)—
(a) for "Charity Commissioners are" substitute " Charity Commission is ", and
(b) for "they" substitute " it ".
Commencement Information
I19. Sch. 8 para. 24 in force at 27.2.2007 by S.I. 2007/309, art. 2, Sch.
25. In section 4 (provisions for protection of existing trusts)—
(a) for "Charity Commissioners" substitute " Charity Commission ", and
(b) in paragraphs (a), (b) and (c) for "they are" substitute " it is ".
Commencement Information
I20. Sch. 8 para. 25 in force at 27.2.2007 by S.I. 2007/309, art. 2, Sch.
26. (1)Section 5 (power to make rules) is amended as follows.
(2) In subsection (1)—
(a) for "Charity Commissioners" substitute " Charity Commission ", and
(b) for "they" substitute " it ".
(3) In subsection (3)—
(a) for "Charity Commissioners" (in both places) substitute " Charity Commission ",
(b) for "they" and "them" (in each place) substitute " it ", and
(c) for "an officer" substitute " a member of staff ".
(4) In the sidenote, for "Charity Commissioners" substitute " Charity Commission ".
Commencement Information
I21. Sch. 8 para. 26 in force at 27.2.2007 by S.I. 2007/309, art. 2, Sch.
27. In section 6. (2) (savings)—
(a) for "Charity Commissioners" substitute " Charity Commission ", and
(b) for "them" substitute " it ".
Commencement Information
I22. Sch. 8 para. 27 in force at 27.2.2007 by S.I. 2007/309, art. 2, Sch.

Green Belt (London and Home Counties) Act 1938 (c. xciii)

28. In section 20 of the Green Belt (London and Home Counties) Act 1938 (lands held on charitable trusts) for "Charity Commissioners" substitute " Charity Commission ".
Commencement Information
I23. Sch. 8 para. 28 in force at 27.2.2007 by S.I. 2007/309, art. 2, Sch.

New Parishes Measure 1943 (No. 1)

29. The New Parishes Measure 1943 has effect subject to the following amendments.
Commencement Information
I24. Sch. 8 para. 29 in force at 27.2.2007 by S.I. 2007/309, art. 2, Sch.
F530. . . . .
Amendments (Textual)
F5. Sch. 8 para. 30 repealed (14.3.2012) by Charities Act 2011 (c. 25), s. 355, Sch. 10 (with s. 20. (2), Sch. 8)
31. In section 31 (charitable trusts)—
(a) for "the Board of Charity Commissioners" substitute " the Charity Commission ", and
(b) for "the Charity Commissioners" substitute " the Charity Commission ".
Commencement Information

I25. Sch. 8 para. 31 in force at 27.2.2007 by S.I. 2007/309, art. 2, Sch.

Crown Proceedings Act 1947 (c. 44)

32. In section 23. (3) of the Crown Proceedings Act 1947 (proceedings with respect to which Part 2 of the Act does not apply) for "Charity Commissioners" substitute " Charity Commission ".
Commencement Information
I26. Sch. 8 para. 32 in force at 27.2.2007 by S.I. 2007/309, art. 2, Sch.

London County Council (General Powers) Act 1947 (c. xlvi)

33. (1)Section 6 of the London County Council (General Powers) Act 1947 (saving for certain trusts) is amended as follows.
(2) In subsection (2)—
(a) for "Charity Commissioners" substitute " Charity Commission ", and
(b) at the end add " ; but this is subject to subsection (3) ".
F6. (3). . . . .
Amendments (Textual)
F6. Sch. 8 para. 33. (3) repealed (14.3.2012) by Charities Act 2011 (c. 25), s. 355, Sch. 10 (with s. 20. (2), Sch. 8)
Commencement Information
I27. Sch. 8 para. 33 in force at 27.2.2007 by S.I. 2007/309, art. 2, Sch.

London County Council (General Powers) Act 1951 (c. xli)

34. In section 33. (6) of the London County Council (General Powers) Act 1951 (improvement of roadside amenities: saving for certain land) for "Charity Commissioners" substitute " Charity Commission ".
Commencement Information
I28. Sch. 8 para. 34 in force at 27.2.2007 by S.I. 2007/309, art. 2, Sch.

City of London (Various Powers) Act 1952 (c. vi)

35. In section 4. (6) of the City of London (Various Powers) Act 1952 (improvement of amenities) for "Charity Commissioners" substitute " Charity Commission ".
Commencement Information
I29. Sch. 8 para. 35 in force at 27.2.2007 by S.I. 2007/309, art. 2, Sch.

City of London (Guild Churches) Act 1952 (c. xxxviii)

36. In section 35 of the City of London (Guild Churches) Act 1952 (saving of rights of certain persons) for "Charity Commissioners" substitute " Charity Commission ".
Commencement Information
I30. Sch. 8 para. 36 in force at 27.2.2007 by S.I. 2007/309, art. 2, Sch.

London County Council (General Powers) Act 1955 (c. xxix)

37. (1)Section 34 of the London County Council (General Powers) Act 1955 (powers as to erection of buildings: saving for certain land and buildings) is amended as follows.
(2) In subsection (2)—

(a) for "Charity Commissioners" substitute " Charity Commission ", and
(b) at the end add " ; but this is subject to subsection (3) ".
F7. (3)................................
Amendments (Textual)
F7. Sch. 8 para. 37. (3) repealed (14.3.2012) by Charities Act 2011 (c. 25), s. 355, Sch. 10 (with s. 20. (2), Sch. 8)
Commencement Information
I31. Sch. 8 para. 37 in force at 27.2.2007 by S.I. 2007/309, art. 2, Sch.

Parochial Church Councils (Powers) Measure 1956 (No. 3)

38. In section 6. (5) of the Parochial Church Councils (Powers) Measure 1956 (consents required for transactions relating to certain property) for "Charity Commissioners" substitute " Charity Commission ".
Commencement Information
I32. Sch. 8 para. 38 in force at 27.2.2007 by S.I. 2007/309, art. 2, Sch.

Recreational Charities Act 1958 (c. 17)

F839................................
Amendments (Textual)
F8. Sch. 8 para. 39 repealed (14.3.2012) by Charities Act 2011 (c. 25), s. 355, Sch. 10 (with s. 20. (2), Sch. 8)
Prospective

Church Funds Investment Measure 1958 (No. 1)

40. Section 5 of the Church Funds Investment Measure 1958 (jurisdiction of Charity Commissioners) is omitted.

Incumbents and Churchwardens (Trusts) Measure 1964 (No. 2)

41. The Incumbents and Churchwardens (Trusts) Measure 1964 has effect subject to the following amendments.
Commencement Information
I33. Sch. 8 para. 41 in force at 27.2.2007 by S.I. 2007/309, art. 2, Sch.
42. In section 2. (3) (property to which Measure applies) for "Charity Commissioners" substitute " Charity Commission ".
Commencement Information
I34. Sch. 8 para. 42 in force at 27.2.2007 by S.I. 2007/309, art. 2, Sch.
43. In section 3. (6) (vesting of property in diocesan authority: saving) for "Charity Commissioners" substitute " Charity Commission ".
Commencement Information
I35. Sch. 8 para. 43 in force at 27.2.2007 by S.I. 2007/309, art. 2, Sch.
44. In section 5 (provisions as to property vested in the diocesan authority) for "Charity Commissioners" substitute " Charity Commission ".
Commencement Information
I36. Sch. 8 para. 44 in force at 27.2.2007 by S.I. 2007/309, art. 2, Sch.
45. (1)The Schedule (procedure where diocesan authority is of the opinion that Measure applies to an interest) is amended as follows.
(2) In paragraph 2 for "Charity Commissioners" substitute " Charity Commission ".

(3) In paragraph 3—
(a) for "Charity Commissioners" substitute " Charity Commission ",
(b) for "they think" (in both places) substitute " it thinks ", and
(c) for "the Commissioners" substitute " the Commission ".
(4) In paragraph 5—
(a) for "Charity Commissioners have" substitute " Charity Commission has ", and
(b) for "they" substitute " it ".
Commencement Information
I37. Sch. 8 para. 45 in force at 27.2.2007 by S.I. 2007/309, art. 2, Sch.

Faculty Jurisdiction Measure 1964 (No. 5)

46. In section 4. (2) of the Faculty Jurisdiction Measure 1964 (sale of books in parochial libraries under a faculty) for "Charity Commissioners" substitute " Charity Commission ".
Commencement Information
I38. Sch. 8 para. 46 in force at 27.2.2007 by S.I. 2007/309, art. 2, Sch.

Industrial and Provident Societies Act 1965 (c. 12)

F9 47. . . . .
Amendments (Textual)
F9. Sch. 8 para. 47 repealed (1.8.2014) by Co-operative and Community Benefit Societies Act 2014 (c. 14), s. 154, Sch. 7 (with Sch. 5)

Clergy Pensions (Amendment) Measure 1967 (No. 1)

48. In section 4. (5) of the Clergy Pensions (Amendment) Measure 1967 (amendments of powers of Board relating to provision of residences) for "Charity Commissioners" and "said Commissioners" substitute " Charity Commission ".
Commencement Information
I39. Sch. 8 para. 48 in force at 27.2.2007 by S.I. 2007/309, art. 2, Sch.

Ministry of Housing and Local Government Provisional Order Confirmation (Greater London Parks and Open Spaces) Act 1967 (c. xxix)

49. In article 11. (3) of the order set out in the Schedule to the Ministry of Housing and Local Government Provisional Order Confirmation (Greater London Parks and Open Spaces) Act 1967 (exercise of powers under articles 7 to 10 of the order) for "Charity Commissioners" substitute " Charity Commission ".
Commencement Information
I40. Sch. 8 para. 49 in force at 27.2.2007 by S.I. 2007/309, art. 2, Sch.

Redundant Churches and other Religious Buildings Act 1969 (c. 22)

F10 50. . . . .
Amendments (Textual)
F10. Sch. 8 paras. 50-52 repealed (14.3.2012) by Charities Act 2011 (c. 25), s. 355, Sch. 10 (with

s. 20. (2), Sch. 8)
F1051. . . . .
Amendments (Textual)
F10. Sch. 8 paras. 50-52 repealed (14.3.2012) by Charities Act 2011 (c. 25), s. 355, Sch. 10 (with s. 20. (2), Sch. 8)
F1052. . . . .
Amendments (Textual)
F10. Sch. 8 paras. 50-52 repealed (14.3.2012) by Charities Act 2011 (c. 25), s. 355, Sch. 10 (with s. 20. (2), Sch. 8)

Children and Young Persons Act 1969 (c. 54)

53. In Schedule 3 to the Children and Young Persons Act 1969 (approved schools and other institutions), in paragraph 6. (3), for "Charity Commissioners" substitute " Charity Commission ".
Commencement Information
I41. Sch. 8 para. 53 in force at 27.2.2007 by S.I. 2007/309, art. 2, Sch.

Synodical Government Measure 1969 (No. 2)

F1154. . . . .
Amendments (Textual)
F11. Sch. 8 paras. 54, 55 repealed (14.3.2012) by Charities Act 2011 (c. 25), s. 355, Sch. 10 (with s. 20. (2), Sch. 8)

Local Government Act 1972 (c. 70)

F1155. . . . .

Consumer Credit Act 1974 (c. 39)

56. In section 16 of the Consumer Credit Act 1974 (exempt agreements), in the table in subsection (3. A) and in subsections (8) and (9), for "Charity Commissioners" substitute " Charity Commission ".
Commencement Information
I42. Sch. 8 para. 56 in force at 27.2.2007 by S.I. 2007/309, art. 2, Sch.

Sex Discrimination Act 1975 (c. 65)

F1257. . . . .
Amendments (Textual)
F12. Sch. 8 para. 57 repealed (14.3.2012) by Charities Act 2011 (c. 25), s. 355, Sch. 10 (with s. 20. (2), Sch. 8)

Endowments and Glebe Measure 1976 (No. 4)

58. The Endowments and Glebe Measure 1976 has effect subject to the following amendments.
Commencement Information
I43. Sch. 8 para. 58 in force at 27.2.2007 by S.I. 2007/309, art. 2, Sch.
F1359. . . . .
Amendments (Textual)

F13. Sch. 8 para. 59 repealed (14.3.2012) by Charities Act 2011 (c. 25), s. 355, Sch. 10 (with s. 20. (2), Sch. 8)
60. In section 18. (2) (means by which land may become diocesan) for "Charity Commissioners" substitute " Charity Commission ".
Commencement Information
I44. Sch. 8 para. 60 in force at 27.2.2007 by S.I. 2007/309, art. 2, Sch.

Interpretation Act 1978 (c. 30)

F1461. . . . .
Amendments (Textual)
F14. Sch. 8 para. 61 repealed (14.3.2012) by Charities Act 2011 (c. 25), s. 355, Sch. 10 (with s. 20. (2), Sch. 8)

Dioceses Measure 1978 (No. 1)

62. The Dioceses Measure 1978 has effect subject to the following amendments.
Commencement Information
I45. Sch. 8 para. 62 in force at 27.2.2007 by S.I. 2007/309, art. 2, Sch.
63. In section 5. (1) (preparation of draft scheme: meaning of "interested parties"), in paragraph (e), for "the Charity Commissioners" substitute " the Charity Commission ".
Commencement Information
I46. Sch. 8 para. 63 in force at 27.2.2007 by S.I. 2007/309, art. 2, Sch.
64. In section 19. (4) (schemes with respect to discharge of functions of diocesan bodies corporate, etc.) for "Charity Commissioners" substitute " Charity Commission ".
Commencement Information
I47. Sch. 8 para. 64 in force at 27.2.2007 by S.I. 2007/309, art. 2, Sch.

Disused Burial Grounds (Amendment) Act 1981 (c. 18)

F1565. . . . .
Amendments (Textual)
F15. Sch. 8 para. 65 repealed (14.3.2012) by Charities Act 2011 (c. 25), s. 355, Sch. 10 (with s. 20. (2), Sch. 8)
Prospective

Local Government (Miscellaneous Provisions) Act 1982 (c. 30)

66. In Schedule 4 to the Local Government (Miscellaneous Provisions) Act 1982 (street trading) for paragraph 1. (2)(j) substitute—
"(j)conducting a public charitable collection that—
(i) is conducted in accordance with section 48 or 49 of the Charities Act 2006, or
(ii) is an exempt collection by virtue of section 50 of that Act."

Administration of Justice Act 1982 (c. 53)

67. In section 41. (1) of the Administration of Justice Act 1982 (transfer of funds in court to official custodian for charities and Church Commissioners) for "Charity Commissioners" substitute " Charity Commission ".
Commencement Information
I48. Sch. 8 para. 67 in force at 27.2.2007 by S.I. 2007/309, art. 2, Sch.

Pastoral Measure 1983 (No. 1)

68. The Pastoral Measure 1983 has effect subject to the following amendments.
Commencement Information
I49. Sch. 8 para. 68 in force at 27.2.2007 by S.I. 2007/309, art. 2, Sch.
F1669............................
Amendments (Textual)
F16. Sch. 8 para. 69 repealed (14.3.2012) by Charities Act 2011 (c. 25), s. 355, Sch. 10 (with s. 20. (2), Sch. 8)
70. In section 63. (4) (trusts for the repair etc. of redundant buildings and contents) for "the Charity Commissioners given under the hand of an Assistant Commissioner" substitute " the Charity Commission ".
Commencement Information
I50. Sch. 8 para. 70 in force at 27.2.2007 by S.I. 2007/309, art. 2, Sch.
71. In section 76. (1) (grant of land for new churches etc. and vesting of certain churches) for "Charity Commissioners" substitute " Charity Commission ".
Commencement Information
I51. Sch. 8 para. 71 in force at 27.2.2007 by S.I. 2007/309, art. 2, Sch.
72. In Schedule 3, in paragraph 11. (1), (2), (6) and (7), for "Charity Commissioners" substitute " Charity Commission ".
Commencement Information
I52. Sch. 8 para. 72 in force at 27.2.2007 by S.I. 2007/309, art. 2, Sch.
Prospective

Rates Act 1984 (c. 33)

F1773............................
Amendments (Textual)
F17. Sch. 8 para. 73 repealed (14.3.2012) by Charities Act 2011 (c. 25), s. 355, Sch. 10 (with s. 20. (2), Sch. 8)

Companies Act 1985 (c. 6)

74. The Companies Act 1985 has effect subject to the following amendments.
Commencement Information
I53. Sch. 8 para. 74 in force at 27.2.2007 by S.I. 2007/309, art. 2, Sch.
Prospective
F1875............................
Amendments (Textual)
F18. Sch. 8 para. 75 repealed (1.10.2009) by The Companies Act 2006 (Consequential Amendments, Transitional Provisions and Savings) Order 2009 (S.I. 2009/1941), art. 1. (2), Sch. 2 (with art. 10)
76. In Schedule 15. D (permitted disclosures of information), in paragraph 21, for "Charity Commissioners to exercise their" substitute " Charity Commission to exercise its ".
Commencement Information
I54. Sch. 8 para. 76 in force at 27.2.2007 by S.I. 2007/309, art. 2, Sch.

Housing Act 1985 (c. 68)

77. (1)Section 6. A of the Housing Act 1985 (definition of "Relevant Authority") is amended as

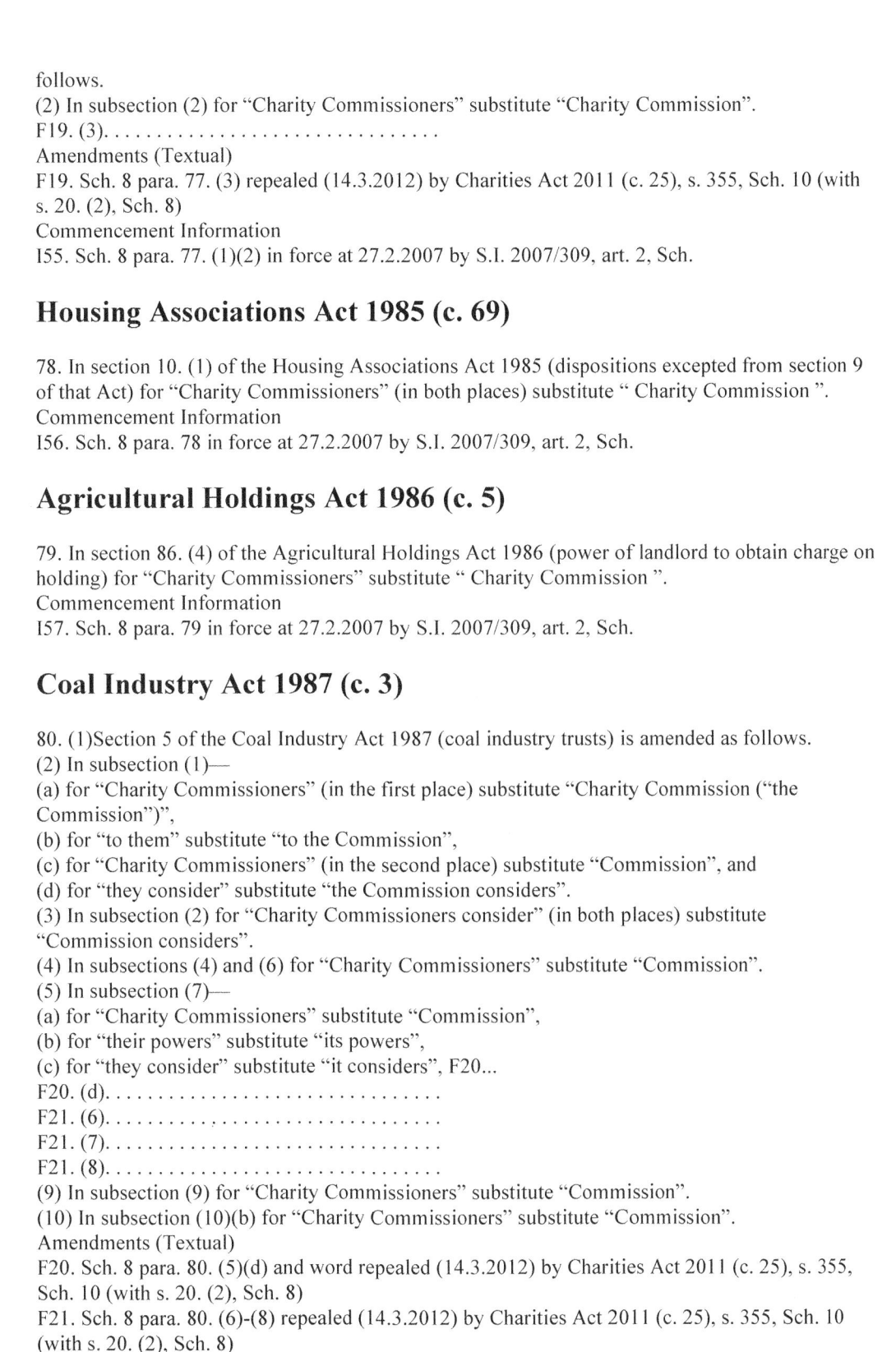

follows.
(2) In subsection (2) for "Charity Commissioners" substitute "Charity Commission".
F19. (3)...............................
Amendments (Textual)
F19. Sch. 8 para. 77. (3) repealed (14.3.2012) by Charities Act 2011 (c. 25), s. 355, Sch. 10 (with s. 20. (2), Sch. 8)
Commencement Information
I55. Sch. 8 para. 77. (1)(2) in force at 27.2.2007 by S.I. 2007/309, art. 2, Sch.

Housing Associations Act 1985 (c. 69)

78. In section 10. (1) of the Housing Associations Act 1985 (dispositions excepted from section 9 of that Act) for "Charity Commissioners" (in both places) substitute " Charity Commission ".
Commencement Information
I56. Sch. 8 para. 78 in force at 27.2.2007 by S.I. 2007/309, art. 2, Sch.

Agricultural Holdings Act 1986 (c. 5)

79. In section 86. (4) of the Agricultural Holdings Act 1986 (power of landlord to obtain charge on holding) for "Charity Commissioners" substitute " Charity Commission ".
Commencement Information
I57. Sch. 8 para. 79 in force at 27.2.2007 by S.I. 2007/309, art. 2, Sch.

Coal Industry Act 1987 (c. 3)

80. (1)Section 5 of the Coal Industry Act 1987 (coal industry trusts) is amended as follows.
(2) In subsection (1)—
(a) for "Charity Commissioners" (in the first place) substitute "Charity Commission ("the Commission")",
(b) for "to them" substitute "to the Commission",
(c) for "Charity Commissioners" (in the second place) substitute "Commission", and
(d) for "they consider" substitute "the Commission considers".
(3) In subsection (2) for "Charity Commissioners consider" (in both places) substitute "Commission considers".
(4) In subsections (4) and (6) for "Charity Commissioners" substitute "Commission".
(5) In subsection (7)—
(a) for "Charity Commissioners" substitute "Commission",
(b) for "their powers" substitute "its powers",
(c) for "they consider" substitute "it considers", F20...
F20. (d)...............................
F21. (6)...............................
F21. (7)...............................
F21. (8)...............................
(9) In subsection (9) for "Charity Commissioners" substitute "Commission".
(10) In subsection (10)(b) for "Charity Commissioners" substitute "Commission".
Amendments (Textual)
F20. Sch. 8 para. 80. (5)(d) and word repealed (14.3.2012) by Charities Act 2011 (c. 25), s. 355, Sch. 10 (with s. 20. (2), Sch. 8)
F21. Sch. 8 para. 80. (6)-(8) repealed (14.3.2012) by Charities Act 2011 (c. 25), s. 355, Sch. 10 (with s. 20. (2), Sch. 8)
Commencement Information

I58. Sch. 8 para. 80. (1)-(5)(9)(10) in force at 27.2.2007 by S.I. 2007/309, art. 2, Sch.

Reverter of Sites Act 1987 (c. 15)

81. The Reverter of Sites Act 1987 has effect subject to the following amendments.
Commencement Information
I59. Sch. 8 para. 81 in force at 27.2.2007 by S.I. 2007/309, art. 2, Sch.
82. (1)Section 2 (Charity Commissioners' schemes) is amended as follows.
(2) In subsection (1) for "Charity Commissioners" substitute " Charity Commission ".
(3) For subsection (3) substitute—
"(3)The charitable purposes specified in an order made under this section on an application with respect to any trust shall be such as the Charity Commission consider appropriate, having regard to the matters set out in subsection (3. A).
(3. A)The matters are—
(a) the desirability of securing that the property is held for charitable purposes ("the new purposes") which are close to the purposes, whether charitable or not, for which the trustees held the relevant land before the cesser of use in consequence of which the trust arose ("the former purposes); and
(b) the need for the new purposes to be capable of having a significant social or economic effect.
(3. B)In determining the character of the former purposes, the Commission may, if they think it appropriate to do so, give greater weight to the persons or locality benefited by those purposes than to the nature of the benefit."
(4) In subsection (5)—
(a) for "Charity Commissioners" substitute " Charity Commission ",
(b) in paragraph (c), for "Commissioners'" and "them" substitute " Commission's " and " it ", and
(c) in paragraph (d), for "Commissioners have" substitute " Commission has ".
(5) In subsection (7) for "Charity Commissioners" substitute " Charity Commission ".
(6) In subsection (8)—
(a) for "Commissioners'" substitute " Commission's ",
(b) for "they think" substitute " it thinks ", and
(c) for "Commissioners decide" substitute " Commission decides ".
(7) In the sidenote, for "Charity Commissioners'" substitute " Charity Commission's ".
Commencement Information
I60. Sch. 8 para. 82. (1)(2)(4)-(7) in force at 27.2.2007 by S.I. 2007/309, art. 2, Sch.
I61. Sch. 8 para. 82. (3) in force at 18.3.2008 by S.I. 2008/751, art. 2, Sch. (with art. 12)
83. (1)Section 4 (provisions supplemental to sections 2 and 3) is amended as follows.
(2) In subsection (1)—
(a) for "Charity Commissioners think" substitute "Charity Commission thinks";
(b) for "Commissioners'" substitute "Commission's"; and
(c) for "the Commissioners think" substitute "the Commission thinks".
F22. (3). . . . .
F22. (4). . . . .
Amendments (Textual)
F22. Sch. 8 para. 83. (3)(4) repealed (14.3.2012) by Charities Act 2011 (c. 25), s. 355, Sch. 10 (with s. 20. (2), Sch. 8)
Commencement Information
I62. Sch. 8 para. 83. (1)(2) in force at 27.2.2007 by S.I. 2007/309, art. 2, Sch.
84. In section 5. (3) (orders under section 554 of the Education Act 1996)—
(a) for "Charity Commissioners" (in both places) substitute " Charity Commission ";
(b) for "the Commissioners" substitute " the Commission "; and
(c) for "them" substitute " it ".

Commencement Information
I63. Sch. 8 para. 84 in force at 27.2.2007 by S.I. 2007/309, art. 2, Sch.

Education Reform Act 1988 (c. 40)

F2385............................
Amendments (Textual)
F23. Sch. 8 paras. 85-88 repealed (14.3.2012) by Charities Act 2011 (c. 25), s. 355, Sch. 10 (with s. 20. (2), Sch. 8)

Courts and Legal Services Act 1990 (c. 41)

F2386............................

London Local Authorities Act 1991 (c. xiii)

F2387............................

Further and Higher Education Act 1992 (c. 13)

F2388............................

Charities Act 1992 (c. 41)

89. The 1992 Act has effect subject to the following amendments.
Commencement Information
I64. Sch. 8 para. 89 in force at 27.2.2007 by S.I. 2007/309, art. 2, Sch.
90. (1)Section 58 (interpretation of Part 2) is amended as follows.
(2) In subsection (1) after the definition of "institution" insert—
""the Minister" means the Minister for the Cabinet Office;".
(3) In subsection (2)—
(a) in paragraph (c) for "to be treated as a promoter of such a collection by virtue of section 65. (3)" substitute "a promoter of such a collection as defined in section 47. (1) of the Charities Act 2006", and
(b) for "Part III of this Act" substitute "Chapter 1 of Part 3 of the Charities Act 2006".
F24. (4)............................
Amendments (Textual)
F24. Sch. 8 para. 90. (4) repealed (14.3.2012) by Charities Act 2011 (c. 25), s. 355, Sch. 10 (with s. 20. (2), Sch. 8)
Commencement Information
I65. Sch. 8 para. 90 partly in force; Sch. 8 para. 90. (2) in force at Royal Assent, see s. 79. (1)(g)
I66. Sch. 8 para. 90. (1)(3) in force at 1.4.2008 by S.I. 2007/3286, art. 3, Sch. 2 (with art. 4)
91. Omit Part 3 (public charitable collections).
Commencement Information
I67. Sch. 8 para. 91 in force at 27.2.2007 by S.I. 2007/309, art. 2, Sch.
92. In section 76. (1) (service of documents) omit paragraph " (c) " and the " and " preceding it.
Commencement Information
I68. Sch. 8 para. 92 in force at 27.2.2007 by S.I. 2007/309, art. 2, Sch.
93. (1)Section 77 (regulations and orders) is amended as follows.
(2) In subsection (1)(b) for "subsection (2)" substitute " subsections (2) and (2. A) ".
(3) After subsection (2) insert—

"(2. A)Subsection (1)(b) does not apply to regulations under section 64. A, and no such regulations may be made unless a draft of the statutory instrument containing the regulations has been laid before, and approved by a resolution of, each House of Parliament."
(4) In subsection (4)—
(a) after "64" insert " or 64. A "; and
(b) omit " or 73 ".
Commencement Information
I69. Sch. 8 para. 93 in force at 27.2.2007 by S.I. 2007/309, art. 2, Sch.
Prospective
94. In section 79 (short title, commencement and extent) omit—
(a) in subsection (6), the words " (subject to subsection (7)) ", and
(b) subsection (7).
Prospective
95. In Schedule 7 (repeals) omit the entry relating to the Police, Factories, &c. (Miscellaneous Provisions) Act 1916 (c. 31).

Charities Act 1993 (c. 10)

F2596............................
Amendments (Textual)
F25. Sch. 8 paras. 96-178 repealed (14.3.2012) by Charities Act 2011 (c. 25), s. 355, Sch. 10 (with s. 20. (2), Sch. 8)
F2597............................
Amendments (Textual)
F25. Sch. 8 paras. 96-178 repealed (14.3.2012) by Charities Act 2011 (c. 25), s. 355, Sch. 10 (with s. 20. (2), Sch. 8)
F2598............................
Amendments (Textual)
F25. Sch. 8 paras. 96-178 repealed (14.3.2012) by Charities Act 2011 (c. 25), s. 355, Sch. 10 (with s. 20. (2), Sch. 8)
F2599............................
Amendments (Textual)
F25. Sch. 8 paras. 96-178 repealed (14.3.2012) by Charities Act 2011 (c. 25), s. 355, Sch. 10 (with s. 20. (2), Sch. 8)
F25100............................
Amendments (Textual)
F25. Sch. 8 paras. 96-178 repealed (14.3.2012) by Charities Act 2011 (c. 25), s. 355, Sch. 10 (with s. 20. (2), Sch. 8)
F25101............................
Amendments (Textual)
F25. Sch. 8 paras. 96-178 repealed (14.3.2012) by Charities Act 2011 (c. 25), s. 355, Sch. 10 (with s. 20. (2), Sch. 8)
F25102............................
Amendments (Textual)
F25. Sch. 8 paras. 96-178 repealed (14.3.2012) by Charities Act 2011 (c. 25), s. 355, Sch. 10 (with s. 20. (2), Sch. 8)
F25103............................
Amendments (Textual)
F25. Sch. 8 paras. 96-178 repealed (14.3.2012) by Charities Act 2011 (c. 25), s. 355, Sch. 10 (with s. 20. (2), Sch. 8)
F25104............................
Amendments (Textual)

F25. Sch. 8 paras. 96-178 repealed (14.3.2012) by Charities Act 2011 (c. 25), s. 355, Sch. 10 (with s. 20. (2), Sch. 8)
F25105.............................
Amendments (Textual)
F25. Sch. 8 paras. 96-178 repealed (14.3.2012) by Charities Act 2011 (c. 25), s. 355, Sch. 10 (with s. 20. (2), Sch. 8)
F25106.............................
Amendments (Textual)
F25. Sch. 8 paras. 96-178 repealed (14.3.2012) by Charities Act 2011 (c. 25), s. 355, Sch. 10 (with s. 20. (2), Sch. 8)
F25107.............................
Amendments (Textual)
F25. Sch. 8 paras. 96-178 repealed (14.3.2012) by Charities Act 2011 (c. 25), s. 355, Sch. 10 (with s. 20. (2), Sch. 8)
F25108.............................
Amendments (Textual)
F25. Sch. 8 paras. 96-178 repealed (14.3.2012) by Charities Act 2011 (c. 25), s. 355, Sch. 10 (with s. 20. (2), Sch. 8)
F25109.............................
Amendments (Textual)
F25. Sch. 8 paras. 96-178 repealed (14.3.2012) by Charities Act 2011 (c. 25), s. 355, Sch. 10 (with s. 20. (2), Sch. 8)
F25110.............................
Amendments (Textual)
F25. Sch. 8 paras. 96-178 repealed (14.3.2012) by Charities Act 2011 (c. 25), s. 355, Sch. 10 (with s. 20. (2), Sch. 8)
F25111.............................
Amendments (Textual)
F25. Sch. 8 paras. 96-178 repealed (14.3.2012) by Charities Act 2011 (c. 25), s. 355, Sch. 10 (with s. 20. (2), Sch. 8)
F25112.............................
Amendments (Textual)
F25. Sch. 8 paras. 96-178 repealed (14.3.2012) by Charities Act 2011 (c. 25), s. 355, Sch. 10 (with s. 20. (2), Sch. 8)
F25113.............................
Amendments (Textual)
F25. Sch. 8 paras. 96-178 repealed (14.3.2012) by Charities Act 2011 (c. 25), s. 355, Sch. 10 (with s. 20. (2), Sch. 8)
F25114.............................
Amendments (Textual)
F25. Sch. 8 paras. 96-178 repealed (14.3.2012) by Charities Act 2011 (c. 25), s. 355, Sch. 10 (with s. 20. (2), Sch. 8)
F25115.............................
Amendments (Textual)
F25. Sch. 8 paras. 96-178 repealed (14.3.2012) by Charities Act 2011 (c. 25), s. 355, Sch. 10 (with s. 20. (2), Sch. 8)
F25116.............................
Amendments (Textual)
F25. Sch. 8 paras. 96-178 repealed (14.3.2012) by Charities Act 2011 (c. 25), s. 355, Sch. 10 (with s. 20. (2), Sch. 8)
F25117.............................
Amendments (Textual)
F25. Sch. 8 paras. 96-178 repealed (14.3.2012) by Charities Act 2011 (c. 25), s. 355, Sch. 10 (with

s. 20. (2), Sch. 8)

F25118..............................

Amendments (Textual)

F25. Sch. 8 paras. 96-178 repealed (14.3.2012) by Charities Act 2011 (c. 25), s. 355, Sch. 10 (with s. 20. (2), Sch. 8)

F25119..............................

Amendments (Textual)

F25. Sch. 8 paras. 96-178 repealed (14.3.2012) by Charities Act 2011 (c. 25), s. 355, Sch. 10 (with s. 20. (2), Sch. 8)

F25120..............................

Amendments (Textual)

F25. Sch. 8 paras. 96-178 repealed (14.3.2012) by Charities Act 2011 (c. 25), s. 355, Sch. 10 (with s. 20. (2), Sch. 8)

F25121..............................

Amendments (Textual)

F25. Sch. 8 paras. 96-178 repealed (14.3.2012) by Charities Act 2011 (c. 25), s. 355, Sch. 10 (with s. 20. (2), Sch. 8)

F25122..............................

Amendments (Textual)

F25. Sch. 8 paras. 96-178 repealed (14.3.2012) by Charities Act 2011 (c. 25), s. 355, Sch. 10 (with s. 20. (2), Sch. 8)

F25123..............................

Amendments (Textual)

F25. Sch. 8 paras. 96-178 repealed (14.3.2012) by Charities Act 2011 (c. 25), s. 355, Sch. 10 (with s. 20. (2), Sch. 8)

F25124..............................

Amendments (Textual)

F25. Sch. 8 paras. 96-178 repealed (14.3.2012) by Charities Act 2011 (c. 25), s. 355, Sch. 10 (with s. 20. (2), Sch. 8)

F25125..............................

Amendments (Textual)

F25. Sch. 8 paras. 96-178 repealed (14.3.2012) by Charities Act 2011 (c. 25), s. 355, Sch. 10 (with s. 20. (2), Sch. 8)

F25126..............................

Amendments (Textual)

F25. Sch. 8 paras. 96-178 repealed (14.3.2012) by Charities Act 2011 (c. 25), s. 355, Sch. 10 (with s. 20. (2), Sch. 8)

F25127..............................

Amendments (Textual)

F25. Sch. 8 paras. 96-178 repealed (14.3.2012) by Charities Act 2011 (c. 25), s. 355, Sch. 10 (with s. 20. (2), Sch. 8)

F25128..............................

Amendments (Textual)

F25. Sch. 8 paras. 96-178 repealed (14.3.2012) by Charities Act 2011 (c. 25), s. 355, Sch. 10 (with s. 20. (2), Sch. 8)

F25129..............................

Amendments (Textual)

F25. Sch. 8 paras. 96-178 repealed (14.3.2012) by Charities Act 2011 (c. 25), s. 355, Sch. 10 (with s. 20. (2), Sch. 8)

F25130..............................

Amendments (Textual)

F25. Sch. 8 paras. 96-178 repealed (14.3.2012) by Charities Act 2011 (c. 25), s. 355, Sch. 10 (with s. 20. (2), Sch. 8)

F25131. . . . .
Amendments (Textual)
F25. Sch. 8 paras. 96-178 repealed (14.3.2012) by Charities Act 2011 (c. 25), s. 355, Sch. 10 (with s. 20. (2), Sch. 8)
F25132. . . . .
Amendments (Textual)
F25. Sch. 8 paras. 96-178 repealed (14.3.2012) by Charities Act 2011 (c. 25), s. 355, Sch. 10 (with s. 20. (2), Sch. 8)
F25133. . . . .
Amendments (Textual)
F25. Sch. 8 paras. 96-178 repealed (14.3.2012) by Charities Act 2011 (c. 25), s. 355, Sch. 10 (with s. 20. (2), Sch. 8)
F25134. . . . .
Amendments (Textual)
F25. Sch. 8 paras. 96-178 repealed (14.3.2012) by Charities Act 2011 (c. 25), s. 355, Sch. 10 (with s. 20. (2), Sch. 8)
F25135. . . . .
Amendments (Textual)
F25. Sch. 8 paras. 96-178 repealed (14.3.2012) by Charities Act 2011 (c. 25), s. 355, Sch. 10 (with s. 20. (2), Sch. 8)
F25136. . . . .
Amendments (Textual)
F25. Sch. 8 paras. 96-178 repealed (14.3.2012) by Charities Act 2011 (c. 25), s. 355, Sch. 10 (with s. 20. (2), Sch. 8)
F25137. . . . .
Amendments (Textual)
F25. Sch. 8 paras. 96-178 repealed (14.3.2012) by Charities Act 2011 (c. 25), s. 355, Sch. 10 (with s. 20. (2), Sch. 8)
F25138. . . . .
Amendments (Textual)
F25. Sch. 8 paras. 96-178 repealed (14.3.2012) by Charities Act 2011 (c. 25), s. 355, Sch. 10 (with s. 20. (2), Sch. 8)
F25139. . . . .
Amendments (Textual)
F25. Sch. 8 paras. 96-178 repealed (14.3.2012) by Charities Act 2011 (c. 25), s. 355, Sch. 10 (with s. 20. (2), Sch. 8)
F25140. . . . .
Amendments (Textual)
F25. Sch. 8 paras. 96-178 repealed (14.3.2012) by Charities Act 2011 (c. 25), s. 355, Sch. 10 (with s. 20. (2), Sch. 8)
F25141. . . . .
Amendments (Textual)
F25. Sch. 8 paras. 96-178 repealed (14.3.2012) by Charities Act 2011 (c. 25), s. 355, Sch. 10 (with s. 20. (2), Sch. 8)
F25142. . . . .
Amendments (Textual)
F25. Sch. 8 paras. 96-178 repealed (14.3.2012) by Charities Act 2011 (c. 25), s. 355, Sch. 10 (with s. 20. (2), Sch. 8)
F25143. . . . .
Amendments (Textual)
F25. Sch. 8 paras. 96-178 repealed (14.3.2012) by Charities Act 2011 (c. 25), s. 355, Sch. 10 (with s. 20. (2), Sch. 8)
F25144. . . . .

Amendments (Textual)
F25. Sch. 8 paras. 96-178 repealed (14.3.2012) by Charities Act 2011 (c. 25), s. 355, Sch. 10 (with s. 20. (2), Sch. 8)
F25145..............................
Amendments (Textual)
F25. Sch. 8 paras. 96-178 repealed (14.3.2012) by Charities Act 2011 (c. 25), s. 355, Sch. 10 (with s. 20. (2), Sch. 8)
F25146..............................
Amendments (Textual)
F25. Sch. 8 paras. 96-178 repealed (14.3.2012) by Charities Act 2011 (c. 25), s. 355, Sch. 10 (with s. 20. (2), Sch. 8)
F25147..............................
Amendments (Textual)
F25. Sch. 8 paras. 96-178 repealed (14.3.2012) by Charities Act 2011 (c. 25), s. 355, Sch. 10 (with s. 20. (2), Sch. 8)
F25148..............................
Amendments (Textual)
F25. Sch. 8 paras. 96-178 repealed (14.3.2012) by Charities Act 2011 (c. 25), s. 355, Sch. 10 (with s. 20. (2), Sch. 8)
F25149..............................
Amendments (Textual)
F25. Sch. 8 paras. 96-178 repealed (14.3.2012) by Charities Act 2011 (c. 25), s. 355, Sch. 10 (with s. 20. (2), Sch. 8)
F25150..............................
Amendments (Textual)
F25. Sch. 8 paras. 96-178 repealed (14.3.2012) by Charities Act 2011 (c. 25), s. 355, Sch. 10 (with s. 20. (2), Sch. 8)
F25151..............................
Amendments (Textual)
F25. Sch. 8 paras. 96-178 repealed (14.3.2012) by Charities Act 2011 (c. 25), s. 355, Sch. 10 (with s. 20. (2), Sch. 8)
F25152..............................
Amendments (Textual)
F25. Sch. 8 paras. 96-178 repealed (14.3.2012) by Charities Act 2011 (c. 25), s. 355, Sch. 10 (with s. 20. (2), Sch. 8)
F25153..............................
Amendments (Textual)
F25. Sch. 8 paras. 96-178 repealed (14.3.2012) by Charities Act 2011 (c. 25), s. 355, Sch. 10 (with s. 20. (2), Sch. 8)
F25154..............................
Amendments (Textual)
F25. Sch. 8 paras. 96-178 repealed (14.3.2012) by Charities Act 2011 (c. 25), s. 355, Sch. 10 (with s. 20. (2), Sch. 8)
F25155..............................
Amendments (Textual)
F25. Sch. 8 paras. 96-178 repealed (14.3.2012) by Charities Act 2011 (c. 25), s. 355, Sch. 10 (with s. 20. (2), Sch. 8)
F25156..............................
Amendments (Textual)
F25. Sch. 8 paras. 96-178 repealed (14.3.2012) by Charities Act 2011 (c. 25), s. 355, Sch. 10 (with s. 20. (2), Sch. 8)
F25157..............................
Amendments (Textual)

F25. Sch. 8 paras. 96-178 repealed (14.3.2012) by Charities Act 2011 (c. 25), s. 355, Sch. 10 (with s. 20. (2), Sch. 8)
F25158. . . . .
Amendments (Textual)
F25. Sch. 8 paras. 96-178 repealed (14.3.2012) by Charities Act 2011 (c. 25), s. 355, Sch. 10 (with s. 20. (2), Sch. 8)
F25159. . . . .
Amendments (Textual)
F25. Sch. 8 paras. 96-178 repealed (14.3.2012) by Charities Act 2011 (c. 25), s. 355, Sch. 10 (with s. 20. (2), Sch. 8)
F25160. . . . .
Amendments (Textual)
F25. Sch. 8 paras. 96-178 repealed (14.3.2012) by Charities Act 2011 (c. 25), s. 355, Sch. 10 (with s. 20. (2), Sch. 8)
F25161. . . . .
Amendments (Textual)
F25. Sch. 8 paras. 96-178 repealed (14.3.2012) by Charities Act 2011 (c. 25), s. 355, Sch. 10 (with s. 20. (2), Sch. 8)
F25162. . . . .
Amendments (Textual)
F25. Sch. 8 paras. 96-178 repealed (14.3.2012) by Charities Act 2011 (c. 25), s. 355, Sch. 10 (with s. 20. (2), Sch. 8)
F25163. . . . .
Amendments (Textual)
F25. Sch. 8 paras. 96-178 repealed (14.3.2012) by Charities Act 2011 (c. 25), s. 355, Sch. 10 (with s. 20. (2), Sch. 8)
F25164. . . . .
Amendments (Textual)
F25. Sch. 8 paras. 96-178 repealed (14.3.2012) by Charities Act 2011 (c. 25), s. 355, Sch. 10 (with s. 20. (2), Sch. 8)
F25165. . . . .
Amendments (Textual)
F25. Sch. 8 paras. 96-178 repealed (14.3.2012) by Charities Act 2011 (c. 25), s. 355, Sch. 10 (with s. 20. (2), Sch. 8)
F25166. . . . .
Amendments (Textual)
F25. Sch. 8 paras. 96-178 repealed (14.3.2012) by Charities Act 2011 (c. 25), s. 355, Sch. 10 (with s. 20. (2), Sch. 8)
F25167. . . . .
Amendments (Textual)
F25. Sch. 8 paras. 96-178 repealed (14.3.2012) by Charities Act 2011 (c. 25), s. 355, Sch. 10 (with s. 20. (2), Sch. 8)
F25168. . . . .
Amendments (Textual)
F25. Sch. 8 paras. 96-178 repealed (14.3.2012) by Charities Act 2011 (c. 25), s. 355, Sch. 10 (with s. 20. (2), Sch. 8)
F25169. . . . .
Amendments (Textual)
F25. Sch. 8 paras. 96-178 repealed (14.3.2012) by Charities Act 2011 (c. 25), s. 355, Sch. 10 (with s. 20. (2), Sch. 8)
F25170. . . . .
Amendments (Textual)
F25. Sch. 8 paras. 96-178 repealed (14.3.2012) by Charities Act 2011 (c. 25), s. 355, Sch. 10 (with

s. 20. (2), Sch. 8)
F25171...............................
Amendments (Textual)
F25. Sch. 8 paras. 96-178 repealed (14.3.2012) by Charities Act 2011 (c. 25), s. 355, Sch. 10 (with s. 20. (2), Sch. 8)
F25172...............................
Amendments (Textual)
F25. Sch. 8 paras. 96-178 repealed (14.3.2012) by Charities Act 2011 (c. 25), s. 355, Sch. 10 (with s. 20. (2), Sch. 8)
F25173...............................
Amendments (Textual)
F25. Sch. 8 paras. 96-178 repealed (14.3.2012) by Charities Act 2011 (c. 25), s. 355, Sch. 10 (with s. 20. (2), Sch. 8)
F25174...............................
Amendments (Textual)
F25. Sch. 8 paras. 96-178 repealed (14.3.2012) by Charities Act 2011 (c. 25), s. 355, Sch. 10 (with s. 20. (2), Sch. 8)
F25175...............................
Amendments (Textual)
F25. Sch. 8 paras. 96-178 repealed (14.3.2012) by Charities Act 2011 (c. 25), s. 355, Sch. 10 (with s. 20. (2), Sch. 8)
F25176...............................
Amendments (Textual)
F25. Sch. 8 paras. 96-178 repealed (14.3.2012) by Charities Act 2011 (c. 25), s. 355, Sch. 10 (with s. 20. (2), Sch. 8)
F25177...............................
Amendments (Textual)
F25. Sch. 8 paras. 96-178 repealed (14.3.2012) by Charities Act 2011 (c. 25), s. 355, Sch. 10 (with s. 20. (2), Sch. 8)
F25178...............................
Amendments (Textual)
F25. Sch. 8 paras. 96-178 repealed (14.3.2012) by Charities Act 2011 (c. 25), s. 355, Sch. 10 (with s. 20. (2), Sch. 8)

Deregulation and Contracting Out Act 1994 (c. 40)

179. (1)Section 79 of the Deregulation and Contracting Out Act 1994 (interpretation of Part 2) is amended as follows.
(2) For subsection (3)(a) substitute—
   "(a)any reference to a Minister included a reference to the Forestry Commissioners or to the Charity Commission;
   (b) any reference to an officer in relation to the Charity Commission were a reference to a member or member of staff of the Commission; and."
(3) In subsection (4) after "those Commissioners" insert " or that Commission ".
Commencement Information
I70. Sch. 8 para. 179 in force at 27.2.2007 by S.I. 2007/309, art. 2, Sch.

Pensions Act 1995 (c. 26)

F26180...............................
Amendments (Textual)
F26. Sch. 8 para. 180 repealed (14.3.2012) by Charities Act 2011 (c. 25), s. 355, Sch. 10 (with s.

20. (2), Sch. 8)

Reserve Forces Act 1996 (c. 14)

181. (1)Schedule 5 to the Reserve Forces Act 1996 (charitable property on disbanding of units) is amended as follows.
(2) In paragraph 1. (2) for "the Charity Commissioners" substitute " the Charity Commission ".
(3) In paragraph 4. (1)—
(a) for "Charity Commissioners consider" substitute " Charity Commission considers ", and
(b) for "they" substitute " it ".
F27. (4)...............................
F27. (5)...............................
Amendments (Textual)
F27. Sch. 8 para. 181. (4)(5) repealed (14.3.2012) by Charities Act 2011 (c. 25), s. 355, Sch. 10 (with s. 20. (2), Sch. 8)
Commencement Information
I71. Sch. 8 para. 181 in force at 27.2.2007 by S.I. 2007/309, art. 2, Sch.

Trusts of Land and Appointment of Trustees Act 1996 (c. 47)

182. In section 6. (7) of the Trusts of Land and Appointment of Trustees Act 1996 (limitation on general powers of trustees) for "Charity Commissioners" substitute " Charity Commission ".
Commencement Information
I72. Sch. 8 para. 182 in force at 27.2.2007 by S.I. 2007/309, art. 2, Sch.

Housing Act 1996 (c. 52)

183. The Housing Act 1996 has effect subject to the following amendments.
Commencement Information
I73. Sch. 8 para. 183 in force at 27.2.2007 by S.I. 2007/309, art. 2, Sch.
184. In section 3. (3) (registration as social landlord) for "Charity Commissioners" substitute " Charity Commission ".
Commencement Information
I74. Sch. 8 para. 184 in force at 27.2.2007 by S.I. 2007/309, art. 2, Sch.
185. In section 4. (6) (removal from the register of social landlords) for "Charity Commissioners" substitute " Charity Commission ".
Commencement Information
I75. Sch. 8 para. 185 in force at 27.2.2007 by S.I. 2007/309, art. 2, Sch.
186. In section 6. (3) (notice of appeal against decision on removal) for "Charity Commissioners" substitute " Charity Commission ".
Commencement Information
I76. Sch. 8 para. 186 in force at 27.2.2007 by S.I. 2007/309, art. 2, Sch.
187. In section 44. (3) (consultation on proposals as to ownership and management of landlord's land) for "Charity Commissioners" substitute " Charity Commission ".
Commencement Information
I77. Sch. 8 para. 187 in force at 27.2.2007 by S.I. 2007/309, art. 2, Sch.
188. In section 45. (4) (service of copy of agreed proposals) for "Charity Commissioners" substitute " Charity Commission ".
Commencement Information
I78. Sch. 8 para. 188 in force at 27.2.2007 by S.I. 2007/309, art. 2, Sch.
189. In section 46. (2) (notice of appointment of manager to implement agreed proposals) for

"Charity Commissioners" substitute " Charity Commission ".
Commencement Information
I79. Sch. 8 para. 189 in force at 27.2.2007 by S.I. 2007/309, art. 2, Sch.
F28190. . . . .
Amendments (Textual)
F28. Sch. 8 para. 190 repealed (1.4.2010) by Housing and Regeneration Act 2008 (c. 17), s. 325. (1), Sch. 16; S.I. 2010/862, art. 3 (with Sch.)
Commencement Information
I80. Sch. 8 para. 190 in force at 27.2.2007 by S.I. 2007/309, art. 2, Sch.
F29191. . . . .
Amendments (Textual)
F29. Sch. 8 para. 191 repealed (14.3.2012) by Charities Act 2011 (c. 25), s. 355, Sch. 10 (with s. 20. (2), Sch. 8)
192. (1)Schedule 1 (regulation of registered social landlords) is amended as follows.
(2) In paragraph 6. (2) (exercise of power to appoint new director or trustee) for "Charity Commissioners" substitute " Charity Commission ".
(3) In paragraph 10 (change of objects by certain charities)—
(a) in sub-paragraphs (1) and (2) for "Charity Commissioners" (in each place) substitute " Charity Commission ", and
(b) in sub-paragraph (2) for "their" substitute " its ".
F30. (4). . . . .
(5) In paragraph 28. (4) (notification upon exercise of certain powers in relation to registered charities) for "Charity Commissioners" substitute " Charity Commission ".
Amendments (Textual)
F30. Sch. 8 para. 192. (4) repealed (14.3.2012) by Charities Act 2011 (c. 25), s. 355, Sch. 10 (with s. 20. (2), Sch. 8)
Commencement Information
I81. Sch. 8 para. 192 in force at 27.2.2007 by S.I. 2007/309, art. 2, Sch. (with art. 12)

School Standards and Framework Act 1998 (c. 31)

F31193. . . . .
Amendments (Textual)
F31. Sch. 8 paras. 193-195 repealed (14.3.2012) by Charities Act 2011 (c. 25), s. 355, Sch. 10 (with s. 20. (2), Sch. 8)
F31194. . . . .
Amendments (Textual)
F31. Sch. 8 paras. 193-195 repealed (14.3.2012) by Charities Act 2011 (c. 25), s. 355, Sch. 10 (with s. 20. (2), Sch. 8)
F31195. . . . .
Amendments (Textual)
F31. Sch. 8 paras. 193-195 repealed (14.3.2012) by Charities Act 2011 (c. 25), s. 355, Sch. 10 (with s. 20. (2), Sch. 8)

Cathedrals Measure 1999 (No. 1)

196. In section 34 of the Cathedrals Measure 1999 (charities) for "Charity Commissioners" substitute " Charity Commission ".
Commencement Information
I82. Sch. 8 para. 196 in force at 27.2.2007 by S.I. 2007/309, art. 2, Sch.

Trustee Act 2000 (c. 29)

197. In section 19. (4) of the Trustee Act 2000 (guidance concerning persons who may be appointed as nominees or custodians) for "Charity Commissioners" substitute " Charity Commission ".
Commencement Information
I83. Sch. 8 para. 197 in force at 27.2.2007 by S.I. 2007/309, art. 2, Sch.

Churchwardens Measure 2001 (No. 1)

F32198. . . . .
Amendments (Textual)
F32. Sch. 8 paras. 198, 199 repealed (14.3.2012) by Charities Act 2011 (c. 25), s. 355, Sch. 10 (with s. 20. (2), Sch. 8)

Licensing Act 2003 (c. 17)

F32199. . . . .

Companies (Audit, Investigations and Community Enterprise) Act 2004 (c. 27)

200. The Companies (Audit, Investigations and Community Enterprise) Act 2004 has effect subject to the following amendments.
Commencement Information
I84. Sch. 8 para. 200 in force at 27.2.2007 by S.I. 2007/309, art. 2, Sch.
201. In section 39 (existing companies: charities), in subsections (1) and (2), for "Charity Commissioners" substitute " Charity Commission ".
Commencement Information
I85. Sch. 8 para. 201 in force at 27.2.2007 by S.I. 2007/309, art. 2, Sch.
202. In section 40 (existing companies: Scottish charities), in subsections (4)(b) and (6), for "Charity Commissioners" substitute " Charity Commission ".
Commencement Information
I86. Sch. 8 para. 202 in force at 27.2.2007 by S.I. 2007/309, art. 2, Sch.
203. In section 54. (7) (requirements for becoming a charity or a Scottish charity)—
(a) for "Charity Commissioners" substitute " Charity Commission ", and
(b) for "their" substitute " its ".
Commencement Information
I87. Sch. 8 para. 203 in force at 27.2.2007 by S.I. 2007/309, art. 2, Sch.
F33204. . . . .
Amendments (Textual)
F33. Sch. 8 paras. 204-207 repealed (14.3.2012) by Charities Act 2011 (c. 25), s. 355, Sch. 10 (with s. 20. (2), Sch. 8)

Pensions Act 2004 (c. 35)

F33205. . . . .
F33206. . . . .
Amendments (Textual)
F33. Sch. 8 paras. 204-207 repealed (14.3.2012) by Charities Act 2011 (c. 25), s. 355, Sch. 10

(with s. 20. (2), Sch. 8)
F33207.................................
Amendments (Textual)
F33. Sch. 8 paras. 204-207 repealed (14.3.2012) by Charities Act 2011 (c. 25), s. 355, Sch. 10 (with s. 20. (2), Sch. 8)

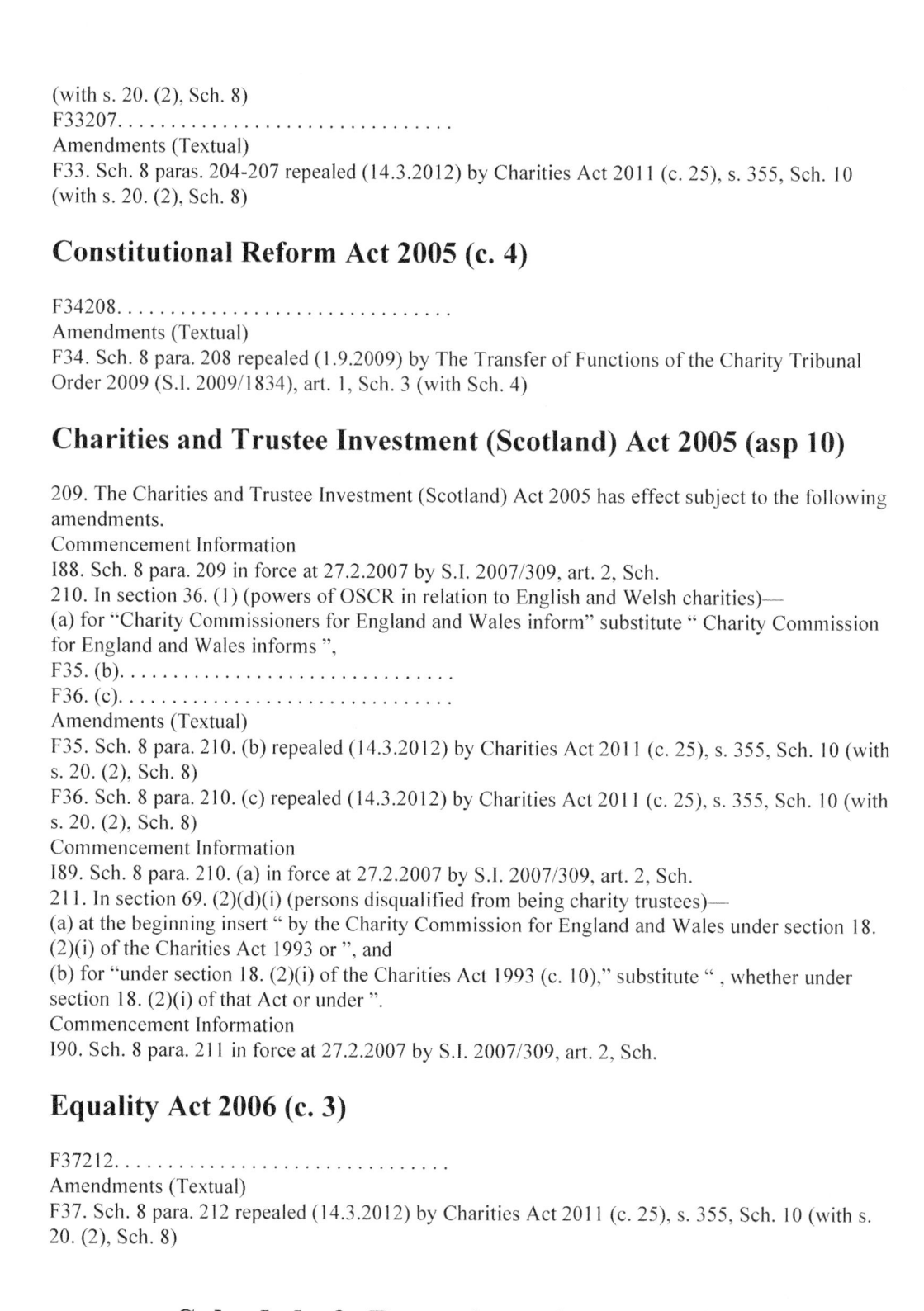

Constitutional Reform Act 2005 (c. 4)

F34208.................................
Amendments (Textual)
F34. Sch. 8 para. 208 repealed (1.9.2009) by The Transfer of Functions of the Charity Tribunal Order 2009 (S.I. 2009/1834), art. 1, Sch. 3 (with Sch. 4)

Charities and Trustee Investment (Scotland) Act 2005 (asp 10)

209. The Charities and Trustee Investment (Scotland) Act 2005 has effect subject to the following amendments.
Commencement Information
I88. Sch. 8 para. 209 in force at 27.2.2007 by S.I. 2007/309, art. 2, Sch.
210. In section 36. (1) (powers of OSCR in relation to English and Welsh charities)—
(a) for "Charity Commissioners for England and Wales inform" substitute " Charity Commission for England and Wales informs ",
F35. (b)................................
F36. (c)................................
Amendments (Textual)
F35. Sch. 8 para. 210. (b) repealed (14.3.2012) by Charities Act 2011 (c. 25), s. 355, Sch. 10 (with s. 20. (2), Sch. 8)
F36. Sch. 8 para. 210. (c) repealed (14.3.2012) by Charities Act 2011 (c. 25), s. 355, Sch. 10 (with s. 20. (2), Sch. 8)
Commencement Information
I89. Sch. 8 para. 210. (a) in force at 27.2.2007 by S.I. 2007/309, art. 2, Sch.
211. In section 69. (2)(d)(i) (persons disqualified from being charity trustees)—
(a) at the beginning insert " by the Charity Commission for England and Wales under section 18. (2)(i) of the Charities Act 1993 or ", and
(b) for "under section 18. (2)(i) of the Charities Act 1993 (c. 10)," substitute " , whether under section 18. (2)(i) of that Act or under ".
Commencement Information
I90. Sch. 8 para. 211 in force at 27.2.2007 by S.I. 2007/309, art. 2, Sch.

Equality Act 2006 (c. 3)

F37212.................................
Amendments (Textual)
F37. Sch. 8 para. 212 repealed (14.3.2012) by Charities Act 2011 (c. 25), s. 355, Sch. 10 (with s. 20. (2), Sch. 8)

Schedule 9. Repeals and revocations

Section 75
Commencement Information

I1. Sch. 9 in force at 27.2.2007 for specified purposes by S.I. 2007/309, art. 2, Sch.
I2. Sch. 9 in force at 28.11.2007 for specified purposes by S.I. 2007/3286, art. 2, Sch. 1
I3. Sch. 9 in force at 18.3.2008 for specified purposes by S.I. 2008/751, art. 2, Sch. (with art. 4)
I4. Sch. 9 in force at 1.4.2008 for specified purposes by S.I. 2008/945, art. 2, Sch. 1 (with arts. 4, 5)
I5. Sch. 9 in force at 31.1.2009 for specified purposes by S.I. 2008/3267, art. 2, Sch. (with arts. 3-27) (as amended: (29.9.2009) by S.I. 2009/2648, art. 3; (26.7.2010) by S.I. 2010/1942, art. 2; and (1.8.2011) by S.I. 2011/1725, arts. 1. (2), 3, Sch. para. 6)
I6. Sch. 9 in force at 30.9.2009 for specified purposes by S.I. 2009/2648, art. 2. (2)(b)
I7. Sch. 9 in force at 1.4.2010 for specified purposes by S.I. 2008/945, art. 2. A, Sch. 1. A (as inserted (30.3.2009) by S.I. 2009/841, art. 2. (2)(6))
I8. Sch. 9 in force at 1.6.2010 for specified purposes by S.I. 2010/503, art. 2, Sch. 1 (with Sch. 2)
I9. Sch. 9 in force at 1.8.2011 for specified purposes by S.I. 2011/1728, art. 2, Sch. 1 (with Sch. 2)

Short title and chapter or title and number | Extent of repeal or revocation |
Police, Factories, &c. (Miscellaneous Provisions) Act 1916 (c. 31) | In section 5(1), in paragraph (b) of the proviso, the words from ", and no representation" onwards. |
Recreational Charities Act 1958 (c. 17) | Section 2. |
Church Funds Investment Measure 1958 (No. 1) | Section 5. |
Charities Act 1960 (c. 58) | The whole Act. |
Housing Act 1985 (c. 68) | In section 6A(5), the words from "and is not" onwards. |
Reverter of Sites Act 1987 (c. 15) | In section 4(4), the words "and appeals" and (in both places) ", and to appeals against,". |
Part 1 (so far as unrepealed).
Part 3.
Section 76. (1)(c) and the word "and" preceding it.
In section 77. (4), "or 73".
In section 79, in subsection (6) the words "(subject to subsection (7))", and subsection (7).
Schedule 5.
In Schedule 6, paragraph 9.
In Schedule 7, the entry relating to the Police, Factories, &c. (Miscellaneous Provisions) Act 1916.
Section 1.
In section 2. (7), the words from ", and the report" onwards.
In section 4, subsection (3) and, in subsection (5), the words ", whether given on such an appeal or not".
Section 6. (9).
Section 9. (4).
In section 16, in subsection (4)(c) the words "in the case of a charity other than an exempt charity,", in subsection (5) the words "which is not an exempt charity and", and subsections (11) to (14).
In section 17. (7), the words from "but this subsection" onwards.
Section 18. (8) to (10).
In section 23. (2), the words "or them".
In section 24. (8), the words from "; and if the scheme" onwards.
Section 28. (10).
In section 33, in each of subsections (2) and (7) the words "(other than an exempt charity)".
Section 44. (3).
Section 46. (8).
Section 61. (7).
In section 73. (4), the words "(other than an exempt charity)".
Section 92.
In section 96, in the definition of "exempt charity" in subsection (1) the words "(subject to section 24. (8) above)", and subsection (4).
Schedule 1.

In Schedule 2, in paragraph (b) the words "and the colleges of Winchester and Eton", and paragraph (x).
In Schedule 6, paragraphs 1. (2), 26, 28 and 29. (2) to (4), (7) and (8).
National Lottery etc. Act 1993 (c. 39) | In Schedule 5, paragraph 12. |
Local Government (Wales) Act 1994 (c. 19) | In Schedule 16, paragraph 99. |
Section 28.
Section 29. (7) and (8).
Housing Act 1996 (c. 52) | In section 58(1)(b), the words from "and is not" onwards. |
Section 41.
In Schedule 3, paragraph 9.
In section 23. (1), the words "which are exempt charities for the purposes of the Charities Act 1993".
In Schedule 30, paragraph 48.
Intervention Board for Agricultural Produce (Abolition) Regulations 2001 (S.I. 2001/3686) | Regulation 6(11)(a). |
Regulatory Reform (National Health Service Charitable and Non-Charitable Trust Accounts and Audit) Order 2005 (S.I. 2005/1074) | Article 3(5). |

Schedule 10. Transitional provisions and savings

Section 75

Section 4: guidance as to operation of public benefit requirement

F11. . . . .
Amendments (Textual)
F1. Sch. 10 paras. 1-14 repealed (14.3.2012) by Charities Act 2011 (c. 25), s. 355, Sch. 10 (with s. 20. (2), Sch. 8)

Section 5: recreational charities etc.

F12. . . . .

Section 18: cy-près schemes

F13. . . . .

Section 19: suspension or removal of trustee etc. from membership of charity

F14. . . . .

Section 20: specific directions for protection of charity

F15. . . . .

Section 26: offence of obstructing power of entry

F16. . . . .

Section 28: audit or examination of accounts of charity which is not a company

F17. . . . .

Section 29: auditor etc. of charity which is not a company to report matters to Commission

F18. . . . .

Section 32: audit or examination of accounts of charitable companies

F19. . . . .

Section 33: auditor etc. of charitable company to report matters to Commission

F110. . . . .

Section 35: waiver of trustee's disqualification

F111. . . . .

Section 36: remuneration of trustees etc. providing services to charity

F112. . . . .

Section 38: relief from liability for breach of trust or duty

F113. . . . .

Section 44: registration of charity mergers

F114. . . . .

Section 67: statements relating to fund-raising

15. The amendments made by section 67 apply in relation to any solicitation or representation to which section 60. (1), (2) or (3) of the 1992 Act applies and which is made on or after the day on which section 67 comes into force.
Commencement Information
I1. Sch. 10 para. 15 in force at 1.4.2008 by S.I. 2007/3286, art. 3, Sch. 2 (with art. 4)

Section 72: Disclosure of information to and by Northern Ireland regulator

16. In relation to an offence committed in England and Wales before the commencement of section 154. (1) of the Criminal Justice Act 2003 (c. 44) (general limit on magistrates' court's power to impose imprisonment), the reference to 12 months in section 72. (6) is to be read as a reference to 6 months.
Commencement Information
I2. Sch. 10 para. 16 in force at 27.2.2007 by S.I. 2007/309, art. 2, Sch.

Schedule 6: group accounts

F217. . . . .
Amendments (Textual)
F2. Sch. 10 paras. 17-20 repealed (14.3.2012) by Charities Act 2011 (c. 25), s. 355, Sch. 10 (with s. 20. (2), Sch. 8)

Schedule 8: minor and consequential amendments

F218. . . . .
F219. . . . .
Amendments (Textual)
F2. Sch. 10 paras. 17-20 repealed (14.3.2012) by Charities Act 2011 (c. 25), s. 355, Sch. 10 (with s. 20. (2), Sch. 8)
F220. . . . .
Amendments (Textual)
F2. Sch. 10 paras. 17-20 repealed (14.3.2012) by Charities Act 2011 (c. 25), s. 355, Sch. 10 (with s. 20. (2), Sch. 8)

Schedule 9: savings on repeal of provisions of Charities Act 1960.

21. (1)This paragraph applies where, immediately before the coming into force of the repeal by this Act of section 35. (6) of the Charities Act 1960 (c. 58) (transfer and evidence of title to property vested in trustees), any relevant provision had effect, in accordance with that provision, as if contained in a conveyance or other document declaring the trusts on which land was held at the commencement of that Act.
(2) In such a case the relevant provision continues to have effect as if so contained despite the repeal of section 35. (6) of that Act.
(3) A "relevant provision" means a provision of any of the following Acts providing for the appointment of trustees—
(a) the Trustee Appointment Act 1850 (c. 28),
(b) the Trustee Appointment Act 1869 (c. 26),
(c) the Trustees Appointment Act 1890 (c. 19), or
(d) the School Sites Act 1852 (c. 49) so far as applying any of the above Acts,
as in force at the commencement of the Charities Act 1960.
Commencement Information
I3. Sch. 10 para. 21 in force at 31.1.2009 by S.I. 2008/3267, art. 2, Sch. (with arts. 3-27) (as amended: (29.9.2009) by S.I. 2009/2648, art. 3; (26.7.2010) by S.I. 2010/1942, art. 2; and (1.8.2011) by S.I. 2011/1725, arts. 1. (2), 3, Sch. para. 6)
22. The repeal by this Act of section 39. (2) of the Charities Act 1960 (repeal of obsolete enactments) does not affect the continued operation of any trusts which, at the commencement of

that Act, were wholly or partly comprised in an enactment specified in Schedule 5 to that Act (enactments repealed as obsolete).

Commencement Information

I4. Sch. 10 para. 22 in force at 31.1.2009 by S.I. 2008/3267, art. 2, Sch. (with arts. 3-27) (as amended: (29.9.2009) by S.I. 2009/2648, art. 3; (26.7.2010) by S.I. 2010/1942, art. 2; and (1.8.2011) by S.I. 2011/1725, arts. 1. (2), 3, Sch. para. 6)

23. The repeal by this Act of section 48. (1) of, and Schedule 6 to, the Charities Act 1960 (consequential amendments etc.) does not affect the amendments made by Schedule 6 in—

F3. (a). . . . .
F3. (b). . . . .
(c) section 24. (4) of the Landlord and Tenant Act 1927 (c. 36), F3...
F3. (d). . . . .

Amendments (Textual)

F3. Sch. 10 para. 23. (a)(b)(d) and word repealed (14.3.2012) by Charities Act 2011 (c. 25), s. 355, Sch. 10 (with s. 20. (2), Sch. 8)

Commencement Information

I5. Sch. 10 para. 23 in force at 31.1.2009 by S.I. 2008/3267, art. 2, Sch. (with arts. 3-27) (as amended: (29.9.2009) by S.I. 2009/2648, art. 3; (26.7.2010) by S.I. 2010/1942, art. 2; and (1.8.2011) by S.I. 2011/1725, arts. 1. (2), 3, Sch. para. 6)

F424. . . . .

Amendments (Textual)

F4. Sch. 10 para. 24 repealed (14.3.2012) by Charities Act 2011 (c. 25), s. 355, Sch. 10 (with s. 20. (2), Sch. 8)

25. Despite the repeal by this Act of section 48. (4) of the Charities Act 1960—

(a) any scheme, order, certificate or other document issued under or for the purposes of the Charitable Trusts Acts 1853 to 1939 and having effect in accordance with section 48. (4) immediately before the commencement of that repeal continues to have the same effect (and to be enforceable or liable to be discharged in the same way) as would have been the case if that repeal had not come into force, and

(b) any such document, and any document under the seal of the official trustees of charitable funds, may be proved as if the 1960 Act had not been passed.

Commencement Information

I6. Sch. 10 para. 25 in force at 31.1.2009 by S.I. 2008/3267, art. 2, Sch. (with arts. 3-27) (as amended: (29.9.2009) by S.I. 2009/2648, art. 3; (26.7.2010) by S.I. 2010/1942, art. 2; and (1.8.2011) by S.I. 2011/1725, arts. 1. (2), 3, Sch. para. 6)

F526. . . . .

Amendments (Textual)

F5. Sch. 10 para. 26 repealed (14.3.2012) by Charities Act 2011 (c. 25), s. 355, Sch. 10 (with s. 20. (2), Sch. 8)

27. The repeal by this Act of the Charities Act 1960 does not affect any transitional provision or saving contained in that Act which is capable of having continuing effect but whose effect is not preserved by any other provision of this Schedule.

Commencement Information

I7. Sch. 10 para. 27 in force at 31.1.2009 by S.I. 2008/3267, art. 2, Sch. (with arts. 3-27) (as amended: (29.9.2009) by S.I. 2009/2648, art. 3; (26.7.2010) by S.I. 2010/1942, art. 2; and (1.8.2011) by S.I. 2011/1725, arts. 1. (2), 3, Sch. para. 6)

Schedule 9: savings on repeal of provisions of Charities Act 1992.

28. The repeal by this Act of section 49 of, and Schedule 5 to, the 1992 Act (amendments relating to redundant churches etc.) does not affect the amendments made by that Schedule in the Redundant Churches and Other Religious Buildings Act 1969.

Commencement Information
I8. Sch. 10 para. 28 in force at 1.4.2008 by S.I. 2008/945, art. 2, Sch. 1 (with arts. 4, 5)

Schedule 9: repeal of certain repeals made by Charities Acts 1960 and 1992.

29. (1)It is hereby declared that (in accordance with sections 15 and 16 of the Interpretation Act 1978 (c. 30)) the repeal by this Act of any of the provisions mentioned in sub-paragraph (2) does not revive so much of any enactment or document as ceased to have effect by virtue of that provision.
(2) The provisions are—
(a) section 28. (9) of the Charities Act 1960 (repeal of provisions regulating taking of charity proceedings),
(b) section 36 of the 1992 Act (repeal of provisions requiring Charity Commissioners' consent to dealings with charity land), and
(c) section 50 of that Act (repeal of provisions requiring amount of contributions towards maintenance etc. of almshouses to be sanctioned by Charity Commissioners).
Commencement Information
I9. Sch. 10 para. 29. (1)(2)(b)(2)(c) in force at 1.4.2008 by S.I. 2008/945, art. 2, Sch. 1 (with arts. 4, 5)
I10. Sch. 10 para. 29. (2)(a) in force at 31.1.2009 by S.I. 2008/3267, art. 2, Sch. (with arts. 3-27) (as amended: (29.9.2009) by S.I. 2009/2648, art. 3; (26.7.2010) by S.I. 2010/1942, art. 2; and (1.8.2011) by S.I. 2011/1725, arts. 1. (2), 3, Sch. para. 6)

Open Government Licence v3.0

Contains public sector information licensed under the Open Government Licence v3.0. The full licence if available at the following address:
http://www.nationalarchives.gov.uk/doc/open-government-licence/version/3/

Printed in Great Britain
by Amazon